CYCLING

COLORADO'S MOUNTAIN PASSES

CYCLING

COLORADO'S MOUNTAIN PASSES

Kurt Magsamen

Fulcrum Publishing
Golden, Colorado

Library of Congress Cataloging-in-Publication Data
Magsamen, Kurt.
  Cycling Colorado's mountain passes / Kurt Magsamen.
      p. cm.
Includes index.
  ISBN 1-55591-294-X (pbk.)
  1. Cycling—Colorado—Guidebooks. 2. Mountain
passes—Colorado—Guidebooks. 3. Colorado—Guidebooks. I.
Title.
  GV1045.5.C6 M34 2002
  796.6′3′09788—dc21

                              2001006697
Printed in Canada
0 9 8 7 6 5 4 3 2 1
Editorial: Kris Fulsaas, Daniel Forrest-Bank
Interior design and formatting: Alice Merrill, Cyndie Chandler
Cover design: Alice Merrill, Nancy Duncan-Cashman
Front cover photograph: Cyclists starting up the east side of
    Independence Pass. Copyright © Kurt Magsamen.
Back cover photograph: Riders topping out on Independence
    Pass. Copyright © Kurt Magsamen.
Maps and graphs: Kurt Magsamen

Fulcrum Publishing
16100 Table Mountain Parkway, Suite 300
Golden, Colorado 80403
(800) 992-2908 • (303) 277-1623
www.fulcrum-books.com

CONTENTS

SOUTH-CENTRAL COLORADO

SOUTHERN COLORADO

INTRODUCTION

The history of cycling is archived in bike shop bathrooms around the world. Faded posters tell the stories of the great ones: Eddy Merckx, Bernard Hinault, Greg LeMond, and now Lance Armstrong summit the great passes of Europe, cheered by thousands, grimacing toward victory. Even for ordinary cyclists, the allure of famous climbs such as Alpe d'Huez is inspiring. Just riding up a road like that is a worthy accomplishment, even if it's not part of a 2,400-mile race. Fortunately, Europe isn't the only place to find inspiring climbs. There are plenty in Colorado.

Colorado's shape is a big box that surrounds the greatest concentration of high peaks in the Lower 48. Beautiful, challenging mountain roads knit this box together, encompassing thirty-eight paved passes ranging in elevation from 9,000 to 12,000 feet. Certainly there are more passes on routes consisting of dirt, rock, or trail and scree, but this book is written for anyone looking for concise, concentrated, and useful information on Colorado's road-bikeable passes.

I've been riding in Colorado for twenty years and, always, the high passes have had a special attraction not unlike the summits of big peaks. The roar of a roadside river, the windblown wildflowers, and the striking change of view as you hit the top are just some of the pleasures that make all the high-altitude grinding worthwhile.

Whenever I wanted to ride a pass, the first source of information was whatever tattered road atlas was at hand. These contain precious little information for a cyclist. How steep is the grade? How sustained? A summit elevation is fine, if it's on the map at all, but what about the starting elevation? How does the western side differ from the eastern side? Whether you're into heart-pounding, lung-burning climbs while imagining that you could have won the Tour after all, or if you're simply interested in getting you and your gear-laden bike to the downhill part, this book provides the kind of detailed information that will help you get more out of your riding time.

This book divides Colorado into four regions—Northern, Central, South-Central, and Southern—and each region contains six to twelve passes. Although the Mount Evans road and Highway 65 near Grand Junction are not really passes, this book includes them because they are two of the biggest hills around. The information included for each pass is intended for cyclists who want to ride either one way to the top and back from either the east or the west, or one way clear across the pass from either east to west or west to east. The recommended start and stop points "bracket" the pass for up to a 100-mile ride (called a century); alternate start and stop points give options for shorter rides. All are intended to be one-day rides.

The rides are described starting from the Front Range (either east or north) side of the pass, with a few exceptions. For instance, Coal Bank and Molas Passes (ride 31) and Red Mountain Pass (ride 32) are described from the south side as part of the San Juan Skyway loop. However, my aim is not to dictate routes or loops, but to provide enough information for you to design your own rides. You can still spread that tattered atlas on the floor and figure out the best three-day ride, or you can bag the passes one at a time, checking them off the list until you've ridden them all.

About This Book

Each pass, as well as the surrounding area, down to 20 to 70 miles from the top in both directions, is described in an overview paragraph, accompanied by an illustrated grade profile and a route map. You'll find concise information summaries for each side of the pass, containing distances (in miles), elevation gains (in feet), grades, and difficulty ratings. Complete

The easy part of Mount Evans—coming down!

stats are given only for the recommended start and stop points. For rides that encompass two passes, elevation gains are listed for the first pass encountered, then the net gain to the second pass (simply the difference in elevation between that pass and the start/stop point) and the total gain to the second pass (which adds on the elevation gain between the two passes).

I had always wondered just what exactly those grade signs on steep roads meant. Percent grade is the rise (elevation gain) over the run (distance)—in the same units—multiplied by 100. A 45-degree angle makes a 100 percent grade. I've calculated the grades given in this book by using USGS topographic maps and topographic software. It is sometimes obvious where the grade changes, but oftentimes not, so I made divisions according to how I think the road feels on a bike. I did not include grades of less than 2 percent. I've also included a maximum grade for each side of each pass. This is the steepest 0.5 mile of the road.

The difficulty ratings range from 1 to 5, 1 being easiest. Very roughly, the difficulty increases with each 1,000 feet of elevation gain. The hardest passes involve about 5,000 feet of climbing; the easiest ones, about 1,000 feet. I've further adjusted the ratings to account for altitude, distance, and my impressions and recollections of the rides.

Each ride begins at a recommended (best) start point on the Front Range (usually east or north) side of the pass; alternate (second- and third-best) start points, if any, are also given. The recommended stop point is described, as well as alternate stop points. There are obviously a lot of ways to ride these roads, but the recommended start and stop points provide easy-to-find references no matter how you're covering the distance. If you want to ride the pass from west to east (or south to north), just reverse the recommended start and stop points. Whether the location is recommended or alternate, its elevation and location are given, as well as distance and elevation gain to the pass—this allows you to quickly compare the stats on each option.

Next you'll find descriptions on road and traffic conditions, including when a road may be closed for the season. The descent to the west is described first, then the descent back down the east side. The Sleep and Supplies section contains information on food and water sources and camping and lodging options, including campsites close to the road or only a short distance on dirt roads. Most public camping is within national forests, on which the Forest Service allows camping nearly anywhere for up to two weeks. I use the Forest Service's term "dispersed camping," by which they mean plopping a tent down nearly anywhere, and I use the term "established camping" for campsites with amenities such as picnic tables, potable water, toilets, and fees. Do not assume that campsites or facilities will be open when you get there; the seasons for them vary quite a bit. I've included phone numbers for the specific National Forest ranger districts so you can call about established campsites; the ranger districts also know about road and weather conditions. For lodging and other services, rather than listing numerous individual establishments, I've kept it simple and included numbers for local chambers of commerce, which are usually eager to help people find what they need. In some cases I've listed where bike supplies are available, but because bike stores fold and start up with great frequency, I haven't tried to list these comprehensively.

Each ride concludes with a mileage log, which can be used as a stand-alone unit that lists specific mileages and landmarks; sometimes I note which side of the highway items are on, but not always, because it's usually obvious. The mileage logs describe each ride from the farthest-east start point to the farthest-west stop point, whether they're an alternate or the recommended start and stop points. This allows you to tailor the ride to your desires, and also shows how each ride can be linked to another. The icons used on the maps and grade profiles (see legend below) are also shown next to the mileage logs, to differentiate between alternate and recommended start/stop points. Again, if you wish to ride the pass in the opposite direction from what is described, just reverse the mileage log.

The mileage logs were compiled from 1998 to 2000. I've tried to include the useful and omit the obvious, but things change, you know; I apologize for any shortcomings in the mileage logs.

Map Legend

● Town or Point of Interest

★ Recommended Starting Point

☆ Alternate Starting Point

▲ Main Pass or High Point

△ Secondary Pass or High Point

⛺ Established Campground

⛺ Possible Dispersed Camping

⛱ Picnic Area

⟶ To Area Off the Map

N

 Compass

Safety

Safety depends on two things: maneuverability and visibility. If either is lacking, you've got problems. Riders who aggressively make themselves maneuverable and visible are safer than riders who passively trust to luck.

So how can you make sure you have maneuverability? First, use as much of the road as you need. When the shoulder is wide, the call is easy, but when the shoulder is stingy or nonexistent, do not yield to too much too soon. A rider too far to the right is obviously in more danger from road hazards but is also in more danger from traffic. How? Most vehicles will try to give a bike enough room, and all the roads in this book are wide enough for traffic to move to the left, but if a vehicle doesn't need to nudge out to the left to pass a cyclist, it won't. The rider far to the right will get passed just as closely as one riding the white line, except that the rider far to the right won't be able to move because there is nowhere to go. If the oncoming vehicle is huge or honking, the cyclist riding the white line can always move over to the right and the vehicle will be able to pass, probably farther left than it would have otherwise, so likely there will be more distance between rider and vehicle.

The second way to ensure maneuverability is to maintain your bike, especially brakes and tires. A blown tire at the wrong time can be disastrous, and knowing that it was due to lousy rim tape or a sloppy job of putting the tube in is hardly consoling.

Visibility, also a twofold safety concern, starts with bright clothing. Road biking is no place for earth tones. The brighter and gaudier, the better. A screamingly loud outfit is as much protection as a helmet. Bright clothing, however, won't make up for a lack of daylight, which is at least predictable. Use lights and reflective gear after dark, or don't ride then.

Storms, however, are not as predictable; they are a severe hazard mostly because they drastically reduce a motorist's visibility. Light rain is one thing, but a heavy cloudburst—so typical in the Rocky Mountains—can make the roads run with water and turn every car into a passing water cannon. Don't ride through a sudden downpour. Get off the road and let it pass. Riding in poor visibility, no matter what the reason, is begging injury.

Weather

Good roads are much more usable in good weather. Fortunately, Colorado has both, mostly. The best weather by far is in autumn. Even though the days are a bit shorter, the weather is so crisp and stable that there is as much pleasant daylight as in summer. Summer's midday heat is a big drag on endurance; autumn makes the long, low flats much more enjoyable to ride. The other good thing about Colorado autumns is that they take a long time to end. Autumn's warm, dry days, so painfully familiar to the ski industry, can stretch from mid-September into November or early December.

Spring is the most frustrating season because it ought to have good weather, but it doesn't. High winds, unstable weather, and tons of snow make riding up high rarely possible.

Summit celebration on Berthoud Pass.

Summer works its way into the high mountains around May or June, and Colorado gets the same weather report until mid-September: hot and dry with afternoon showers. Afternoon showers can at least be avoided. Unlike hikers or other outdoor folks, a bicyclist can outrun or avoid thundershowers because they are so local. The old hiker's axiom of reaching the top by noon will work to escape thundershowers, but for cyclists it will invite a day of head winds.

The general summer wind pattern in the mountains is light winds moving downhill first, in the early morning, and then the winds reversing and heading back uphill by midmorning. When the air is cool enough in the early morning, it pours down. When it gets heated up, it flows back upward and starts making cumulus clouds. When and how much this happens depends on many things—relative temperatures, altitude of the valley, the angle of the sun—but I generally notice uphill winds starting about 9:00 A.M. They are not usually strong, but even a light head wind can negate a light downhill grade, especially when dropping into hot areas such as the San Luis Valley or east of the Front Range. Starting later in the day will subject you to higher temperatures and greater risk from thunderstorms, but better winds—tailwinds for heading up toward a pass.

Conditioning

Most recreational cyclists train for distance, not speed. The goal is usually a 100-mile one-day ride or a several hundred–mile tour over a few days, and it makes sense to build miles at whatever rate time will allow.

One of the best additions to distance training is interval training. Intervals mix short periods of hard riding with rest periods, which develops power and cardiovascular fitness. Some extra power and better use of the air you breathe is exactly what's needed in those last few miles to the top of any pass. Riding strongly near the summit will add a lot to your endurance, too, because nothing kills endurance like a long grind at less than 10 miles per hour. One of the biggest advantages of interval training, however, is not on the road but at home. Long rides that push the 60-mile mark are tough to fit into the middle of the week. Intervals allow more intense workouts that can be done in an hour or less and are easier to work into a practical schedule.

Besides improving power and endurance, try conserving them. One of the best ways to do this is by developing a good spin speed. A cadence (pedal revolutions per minute) of around 90 rpm will not only conserve power but help prevent injury. Intervals and cadence work can be done with nothing but a watch, although a cyclo-computer with cadence is immensely helpful.

Gear

It's difficult in any sport to get the right gear for the right conditions, especially when you're starting out. No one can tell you what's perfect for you, but here are a few suggestions for adapting the gear you may have and expanding your riding options without buying a stable of bikes and a closet of gear.

A well-cared for bike mounted properly on a bike rack.

Bicycle

Nothing is better for riding on roads than a road bike, and this book is written with road bikes in mind. If you've got only a mountain bike, then put on 1-inch-wide tires and pump the pressure up to about 80 pounds per square inch. Get slick or mostly smooth tires. On pavement, knobby tires increase rolling resistance and actually decrease traction. The next best way to "roadify" a mountain bike is to swap the suspension fork for a simple rigid one. This, admittedly, is more costly than a tire change but will save weight. Some might assume that when hills are involved, the lower the gearing, the better. Most modern road bikes are geared with a 39-tooth small chain ring up front and about a 27-tooth cog as the largest in back. This is fine for any of the roads in this book. Mountain bike gearing is great for trails but too low (slow) for these roads.

Carrying Capacity

One of the most efficient ways to ride a lot of passes is to do a few on a single multiday tour, but staying out a long time means carrying gear, and many road bikes are not well suited to hauling. Most road bikes, especially nice racing ones, have short wheel bases and no braze-ons for rack and pannier attachments. Does this mean you're limited to one-day rides or tours supported by a SAG wagon? Not if you get a trailer.

Trailers have a lot of advantages over panniers, not the least of which is that you can use them with any bike without marring or modifying the bicycle itself. Any bike—mountain, racing, touring, even a cruiser—can take a trailer. You can also carry just about anything in them without worrying about   balancing the weight or breaking spokes from overloading. Because trailers have such a large carrying capacity, stronger riders can carry more, weaker riders can carry less and thus keep up with the stronger riders: Everyone can ride together. Disconnect a trailer, and you've got your regular bike back. A trailer is the most cost-effective way to expand the uses of any bike.

Another useful invention is the quick-release beam rack. A beam rack is just a tube (the beam) supporting a small platform for gear. The whole thing clamps onto the seat post with no need for braze-ons. Like trailers, they fit easily onto most bikes and will allow you to carry extra clothes, food, or a camera without bulging jersey pockets. This is useful for even the most lightweight credit-card tour.

Clothing

An adaptable bike is useful, but adaptable clothing is essential. Even if the weather doesn't change, conditions will for a cyclist. Riding up a long hill can be hot, sweaty work, and a downhill at 30 or 40 miles per hour means a sudden chill. Even on the hottest days, a light coat is well worthwhile. Your basic clothing kit for good weather should include:

❑ helmet
❑ gloves
❑ jersey
❑ cycling shorts
❑ cycling shoes
❑ sunglasses
❑ sunscreen
❑ light jacket

Earlier or later in the season, if you want to keep riding in the mountains, add:

❑ tights
❑ booties
❑ Windstopper gloves
❑ hat that fits under the helmet and keeps your ears warm
❑ three-ply Gore-Tex coat

Windstopper fleece and other such material works well if worn up front where the wind is, but not in back. Too much Windstopper will prevent your sweat from being wicked away from your body. Lighter-weight Gore-Tex shells are preferable because they pack much easier, breathe easier, are waterproof in all but torrential conditions, and are less expensive. Non-breathable shells are next to worthless. If you use a jacket with a hood, be sure the hood moves with your head. A poorly fitting hood will compromise peripheral vision.

Tools

The only other essentials are a few tools. Always take:

❑ pump
❑ tire levers
❑ patch kit
❑ at least one spare tube
❑ micro tool with Allen keys and screwdrivers
❑ small pocket knife
❑ money

Fill up the water bottles and quit reading that guidebook already.

NORTHERN COLORADO

1   CAMERON PASS
10,276 feet

The most difficult thing about riding up Cameron Pass from the east side is distance, not steepness. From the junction of Colorado Highway 14 and U.S. Highway 287 (the junction known as Ted's Place), it is 57 miles west to Cameron Pass and more than 5,000 feet up. The grade on the eastern side rarely and only briefly exceeds 3 percent in the first 45 miles, and for this reason the recommended ride doesn't include the whole climb. Riding from the Tunnel Picnic Area to Gould and back is the best part of Colorado Highway 14 at Cameron Pass. The Poudre Canyon, between Ted's Place and Cameron Pass, is an immensely popular recreation area replete with campsites and picnic grounds; the benefit of its popularity is that all the facilities make for a flexible ride. It's easy to pick a distance and find a nearby parking lot for an alternate start. The ride up the western side of Cameron Pass is steeper and uncrowded but short, rising 1,256 feet in 8 miles.

EAST TO WEST: Distance from Ted's Place to Walden: 87.5 miles

EAST SIDE: Distance from Tunnel Picnic Area to summit: 12.2 miles

Elevation gain: 2,236 feet

Grades: Maximum 6.0%; 3.3% for 6 miles, 4.7% for 4.4 miles

Difficulty: 2

WEST SIDE: Distance from Moose Visitors Center to summit: 8 miles

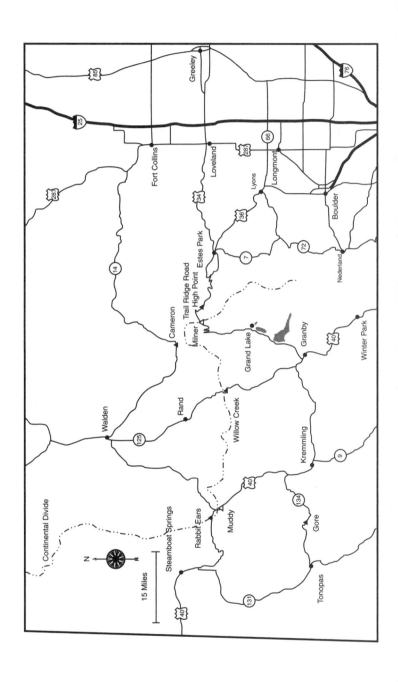

Elevation gain: 1,256 feet
Grades: Maximum 5%; average 2% for 4.3 miles, 4.4% for 3.75
    miles
Difficulty: 1

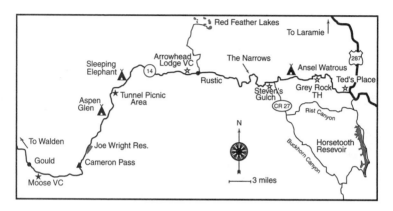

Recommended Start and Stop Points

East Side: Tunnel Picnic Area (8,040 feet), a small spot on
the south side of Highway 14, 44.8 miles west of Ted's Place;
12.2 miles and 2,236 feet of elevation gain to Cameron Pass.
Tunnel Picnic Area is difficult to see because it is a small spot
below the road next to the Poudre River. A short gravel road
leads to several tables and some toilets. Starting from here
maximizes the best and minimizes the worst of the Poudre
Canyon. From here to the top, the road surface is excellent
and there is at least a 2-foot shoulder. This high up the canyon,
traffic is merely ordinary. This is also a good place from which
to ride both sides of the pass (from here, the grade steepens and
the road is wide and excellent), turning around at the Moose
Visitors Center on the west side for a 40.6-mile out-and-back.
Note: Do not confuse the Tunnel Picnic Area with the small
tunnel 14.4 miles west of Ted's Place; they have only a name in
common.

West Side: Colorado State Forest State Park Moose Visitors
Center (9,020 feet), on the south side of Highway 14, 8 miles
west of Cameron Pass; 8 miles and 1,256 feet of elevation gain to

Approaching Cameron Pass from the west.

Cameron Pass. This log building with a blue steel roof is almost as big as its name; inside are friendly, counter-bound rangers, dioramas, maps, and books to buy. It is surrounded by a huge parking lot. Rest rooms and water are available but no food; the town of Gould is 1 mile west, and sodas and candy may be had at a KOA campground 3.25 miles west. From the visitors' center, it's pleasant riding to the summit.

Alternate Start and Stop Points

East Side: Ted's Place (5,220 feet), junction of U.S. Highway 287 and Colorado Highway 14, 57 miles and 5,056 feet of elevation gain to Cameron Pass. Because Ted's Place is a staging area for rafting companies that work in the Poudre Canyon, there is a large gas station with large supplies of gas and junk food, and a lot of parking. In the afternoon, you'll share space with busloads of rafters. There are bathrooms, tables, and even changing booths. There is also an information sign with a map of the canyon and all its campsites and facilities.

Grey Rock Trailhead (5,560 feet), on the left side of Highway 14, 8.2 miles from Ted's Place; 48.8 miles and 4,716 feet of elevation gain to Cameron Pass. This is the best place to start if you'd like to make an out-and-back to Cameron Pass a century. There are rest rooms at this parking lot but nothing else. Despite its size, the place fills up fast on weekends.

Poudre Park Picnic Area (5,700 feet), on the right side of Highway 14, 11 miles west of Ted's Place; 46 miles and 4,576 feet of elevation gain to Cameron Pass. If Grey Rock is crowded, chances are you can still get a spot at Poudre Park. Facilities are better, and food is available in the town of Poudre Park 1 mile before the picnic area.

Steven's Gulch Day Use Area (6,120 feet), on the right side of Highway 14, 17 miles west of Ted's Place; 40 miles and 4,156 feet of elevation gain to Cameron Pass. This is a good place to start if you'd like to ride through The Narrows—a tight, winding section of road that is the most interesting of the lower canyon. Even though the ride is shortened, the day will still be long.

Arrowhead Lodge Visitors Center (7,400 feet), on the right side of Highway 14, 33.7 miles west of Ted's Place, up the canyon just beyond the town of Rustic; 23.4 miles and 2,876 feet of elevation gain to Cameron Pass. This is the visitors' center for Arapaho National Forest. There is some parking here, and the visitors' center has standard facilities, rest rooms, and a few displays and maps. This makes a good halfway point. The road and traffic improve from here on up because nearly all the residences are east of here.

Road and Traffic Conditions

The shoulder on Colorado Highway 14 is intermittent to nonexistent for the first 35 miles west of Ted's Place. Typically, the tightest curves have the smallest shoulders. Traffic in the Poudre Canyon is bad. On any summer day there are hikers, rafters, fishermen, campers, RVs, mountain bikers, and trucks all vying for space on a two-lane roadway. Parking lots near trailheads overflow and cars park along the roadway, making a narrow road even narrower. If you ride the lower part of the canyon on a weekend afternoon, expect close encounters with long lines of frustrated motorists. The good thing about Poudre Canyon is that the farther up you go the better the road and the traffic become. Starting from the Tunnel Picnic Area, there is much less traffic and a beautiful 2-foot shoulder all the way to Gould, about a mile past Moose Visitors Center.

Descents

West Side: The road is good, the shoulder generous, and the curves gentle. Unfortunately it ends too soon, and before long you'll be coasting down forested flats on the way to Walden.

East Side: The descent is steep near the top; you rock and rocket through gentle curves all the way to the Tunnel Picnic Area. Beyond here, the road flattens out and you'll have to work to get to Ted's Place. The gentle grade makes it a great place to spin in the big ring, but even a slight head wind counters the grade and makes the day a grind. The only exciting curves are in The Narrows.

Sleep and Supplies

It is not difficult to travel lightly in the Poudre Canyon; it has more campsites and picnic areas than any other canyon in the state. Food is available at the convenience store at Ted's Place, the towns of Poudre Park and Rustic, a general store (chips, soda, candy bars) 43 miles east of Ted's Place, the town of Gould (one restaurant), KOA campground 2.3 miles west of Gould (sodas, candy), and Walden. Campgrounds have drinking water, but picnic areas and trailheads do not. The nearest bike stores are in Fort Collins, on U.S. Highway 287 southeast of Ted's Place. For more information, call the Fort Collins Convention and Visitors Bureau, 800-274-3678, for east of Cameron Pass, or the North Park Chamber, 970-723-4600, for west of the pass.

The eastern side of the pass is almost entirely within Roosevelt National Forest. Information is available from the U.S. Forest Service Visitors Information Center, 970-498-2770, or the Estes Park-Poudre/Red Feather Ranger Districts, 970-498-2775. Forest Service campsites in Poudre Canyon are

Ansel Watrous, The Narrows, Sleeping Elephant, Aspen Glen, Stove Prairie, Mountain Park, Big Bend, and Big South. Ansel Watrous and Big Bend are open year-round, but the others are generally open from spring to fall. Camping is restricted to campsites from mile 6 through 49. Day-use areas are officially open from 10:00 A.M. to 6:00 P.M. Signs explaining rules and fees are everywhere.

The western side of the pass is part of Colorado State Parks, 970-226-6641. The Ranger Lakes State Campground is 2.5 miles east of the Moose Visitors Center.

MILEAGE LOG

☆0.0 Ted's Place, junction of U.S. Highway 287 and Colorado Highway 14. Gas station and convenience store, picnic tables, rest rooms, plenty of parking, pay phones, even stalls to change clothes.

2.6 Picnic Rock Picnic Area. Tables and rest rooms.

3.0 Poudre River Visitor Information Center pullout on the right, with a large sign describing the canyon and maps of the canyon that point out the locations of all facilities.

5.0 Steep section near Waterworks, on the right. A pullout is just after the Waterworks utility turnoff.

6.0 Sign on the right reads "No camping within ¼ mile of

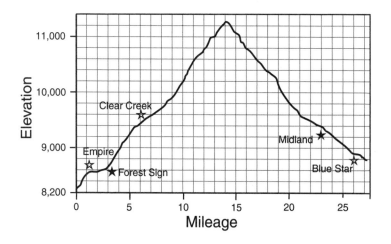

river next 43 miles except in designated areas."

7.0 Parking area on the right.

☆8.2 Grey Rock Trailhead on the left. Large parking area for this popular trailhead. The round trip from here to Cameron Pass and back is just under 100 miles.

9.5 Poudre Park, the first small town in the canyon. Little here except a small gas station and grocery store, which may or may not be open.

☆11.0 Poudre Park Picnic Area on the right. Two picnic tables near the river.

12.3 Ansel Watrous Campground on the right.

12.6 Young's Gulch Trailhead. Parking may be limited. Young's Gulch is a popular mountain bike ride.

13.8 The Mishawaka, a small bar with good music and views of the river. Bar food available; parking is tight, especially during shows.

14.4 A short tunnel through a rock buttress. Note that this is not the Tunnel Picnic Area.

15.9 County Road 27, the Stove Prairie road, recently paved, to the left. Enough room to park here (also provides access to the Stove Prairie road).

☆17.0 Steven's Gulch Day Use Area. Beginning of The Narrows, a 2.5-mile stretch of twisting road through tight walls with 20 mph curves. In spring and autumn, expect gravel left over from road sanding.

21.5 Century Park Day Use Area, close to the river. Picnic tables, rest rooms; this is also a good alternate start but you'll miss The Narrows.

25.7 County Road 63e, the Pingree Park Road, on the left.

30.0 Indian Meadows Lodge and restaurant.

30.7 Rustic, the second small town in the canyon. Gas station and restaurant. The Red Feather Lakes road is on the right.

☆33.7 Arrowhead Lodge, Arapaho National Forest Visitors Center, on the right. Here's another place to learn all about the canyon, and another good alternate starting point.

39.0 Big Bend Campground and Picnic Area on the left.

43.1 General Store, with a small collection of cabins.

★45.0 Tunnel Picnic Area on the left. The picnic area is hard to see, down a small dirt road about 50 yards.

48.8 Big South Trailhead on the left, another possible starting point.

50.3 Larimer County Road 103, the Glendevy Road.

52.3 Blue Lake Trailhead.

54.3 Parking for Joe Wright Reservoir on the left.

55.5 Zimmerman Lake Trailhead.

▲57.1 Cameron Pass, elevation 10,276 feet. Spacious picnic area on the right with plenty of parking.

59.2 Lake Agnes Campground and American Lakes Trailhead. Good view of the Noku Crags to the south.

61.0 Road flattens out.

62.5 Ranger Lake Campground and Colorado State Forest Headquarters.

65.3 Large parking area signed "Recreational Parking" on the left.

★65.0 Colorado State Forest State Park Moose Visitors Center on the left.

66.0 The town of Gould.

68.3 Colorado State Forest campground area and KOA camping.

☆87.5 Walden.

2   RABBIT EARS PASS
9,426 feet

Rabbit Ears Pass provides an excellent road with a variety of difficulties and terrain. The eastern side is steep but short, offering long views over North Park. As with other northern passes, getting to the top is not the end of your effort. The summit plateau between Rabbit Ears Pass and West Summit is about 8 miles long and prone to northern and westerly winds. The high point on the road is 9,500 feet, a few feet higher than the actual pass. The western side is a rocket ride down—and, conversely, an unrelenting grind up. The two sides could not be more different as far as facilities go. There is nothing near the beginning of the eastern grade, so you'll have to park off the road, which makes the eastern approach even longer. On the west side, Steamboat Springs, being a ski town, has a surfeit of facilities.

EAST TO WEST: Distance from Muddy Pass Lake to Lincoln Park in Steamboat Springs: 24.7 miles

EAST SIDE: Distance from Muddy Pass Lake to Rabbit Ears Pass: 2.3 miles; to west summit, 10 miles

Elevation gain: 626 feet

Grades: Maximum 5.4%; average 4.4% for 2.3 miles

Difficulty: 1

WEST SIDE: Distance from Lincoln Park in Steamboat Springs to Rabbit Ears Pass: 22.4 miles

Elevation gain: 2,775 feet

Grades: Maximum 7.3%; average 0.6% for 6.4 miles, 6.4% for 7.2 miles, 0–7% for 7.6 miles

Difficulty: 3

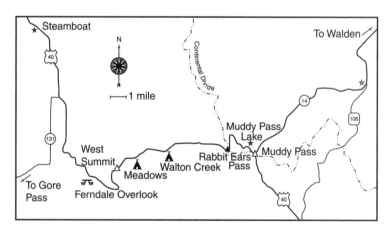

Recommended Start and Stop Points

East Side: Muddy Pass Lake (8,800 feet), on the right (north) side of U.S. Highway 40, 0.5 mile west of Muddy Pass; 2.3 miles and 626 feet of elevation gain to Rabbit Ears Pass. This popular fishing spot with plenty of space to park is much more pleasant than any other nearby starting places to the east. The only disadvantage is that Rabbit Ears Pass is reached in only 2.3 miles of riding, but this is easily remedied by riding to Steamboat Springs and back, a total of 49.4 miles.

West Side: Lincoln Park (6,725 feet), a block south of Main and Twelfth in Steamboat Springs; 22.4 miles and a tough 2,775 feet of elevation gain to Rabbit Ears Pass. There are tables and rest rooms along the river, all in easy walking distance to everything in Steamboat.

Alternate Start and Stop Points

East Side: Forest Road 106 (8,500 feet) on the left side of Colorado Highway 14, 10 miles east of Muddy Pass Lake; 12.3 miles and 926 feet of elevation gain to Rabbit Ears Pass. This is the best alternative for warming up on the flat before hitting the mountain. The ride from here is scenic, and the road is newly resurfaced with a 1-foot shoulder. Forest Road 106 is the road to Indian Creek. Between this junction and the recommended start at Muddy Pass Lake, there are large signs giving mileages to various roads and peaks. The signs are usually impossible to read because they're shot to hell. This intersection is on Bureau of Land Management land. Note: The mileage log doesn't include this or the next alternate start/stop point because they come from different directions.

Pullout (8,000 feet) near mile 166 on U.S. Highway 40, 8.3 miles south of Muddy Pass Lake. If you're coming from the south and would like to ride the entire eastern side of Rabbit Ears Pass, park at this pullout before Muddy Pass. Note: The mileage log doesn't include this or the preceding alternate start/stop point because they come from different directions.

West Side: Easternmost shopping complex (6,700 feet) just east of Steamboat Springs off Mount Werner Drive; 19.4 miles and 2,726 feet of elevation gain to Rabbit Ears Pass. You can cut out some traffic lights and tourist traffic in Steamboat by starting at any of the strip malls just east of town. They feature massive parking lots and every sort of food and drink (gas, groceries, coffee, liquor, spas).

Road and Traffic Conditions

U.S. Highway 40 from Muddy Pass to Steamboat is a relatively new road, and the steepest sections are three luxurious lanes wide. There's plenty of room for a bike, and the good surface encourages speed. Weekend traffic is heavy all day. Steamboat hosts car and motorcycle conventions, so the road is sometimes crowded with Mustangs or Harleys. U.S. Highway 40 from Kremmling to Muddy Pass is a miserable road. It's hot and might as well be a two-lane interstate for as fast as the traffic goes. Colorado Highway 14 from Forest Road 106 to Muddy Pass is 9.2 miles.

Descents

West Side: The fastest road in northern Colorado. The grade is a sustained 7 percent, and none of the curves are sharp enough to slow down for, even at 40-plus miles per hour. A wide, clean, smooth road makes speed all the easier. Approaching 50 miles per hour, it is tempting to move into a car lane. This is risky because downhill traffic is also very fast, usually faster than 70 miles per hour.

East Side: The straightaways are up top and the curves are down low. Neither section lasts long and together they are too little of a good thing.

Sleep and Supplies

The eastern side of Rabbit Ears Pass is far from anything—Walden is 34 miles east of Muddy Pass via Colorado Highway 14; Kremmling is 27 miles south of Muddy Pass via U.S. Highway 40. Steamboat Springs is the supply point of choice for this area. There is even a bike store, the Sore Saddle Cyclery, south of Main and Twelfth Streets near the riverside Lincoln Park. For more information, call the North Park Chamber of Commerce, 970-723-4600, east of the pass or the Steamboat Chamber of Commerce, 970-879-0882, west of the pass.

The summit plateau is in Routt National Forest, 970-879-1870. Campgrounds are in the Hahns Peak/Bear Ears Ranger District, 970-879-1870. The two near the road are Walton Creek and Meadows.

MILEAGE LOG

★0.0 Muddy Pass Lake (8,800 feet). Plenty of room to park.

▲2.3 Rabbit Ears Pass (9,426 feet). Large parking spaces on either side of the pass. The road goes up a bit as it continues rolling west.

2.7 Muddy Creek Road 312 on the right and Buffalo Park Road 100 to the left. Both of these roads lead to good camping.

6.2 Trailhead parking to the south. Begin going down, but you're not to the western summit yet.

6.6 Walton Creek Campground.

7.2 Trailhead parking to the north.

7.8 Meadows Campground.

8.3 Pullout for Bruce's trail on the north.

△9.9 Rabbit Ears Pass West Summit (9,400 feet). Parking areas provide a place to check brakes, plus more trail access.

12.6 The heart of the downhill, two lanes.

13.5 Ferndale overlook and picnic area on the right.

17.2 Routt County Road 20.

17.4 The grade ends abruptly here. Cruise into Steamboat.

20.0 Junction with Colorado Highway 131 to the left heading south; continue on Highway 14. Sign says "Steamboat 4."

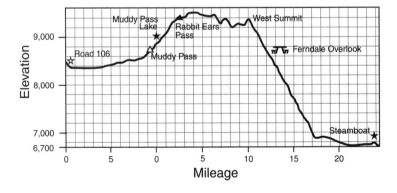

21.3 Forest Service information center.

☆21.9 Turnoff for Mount Werner Road at a giant strip-mall complex (6,700 feet on the right).

22.8 Angler's Drive; City Information Booth. Information on Steamboat and nothing else.

24.4 Intersection of Main and Ninth Streets. Yampa River picnicking and fishing to the left.

★24.7 Intersection of Main and Twelfth Streets; follow the signs to Lincoln Park (6,725 feet). There is a good area between the bike store and the river for gearing up or hanging out.

3   TRAIL RIDGE ROAD
12,183 feet

Trail Ridge Road was designed to be spectacular, not efficient. Most mountain roads crawl up a canyon and poke over the mountains at the lowest point. Trail Ridge Road gains a high alpine ridge in Rocky Mountain National Park and stays on it for as long as possible. This high section is a fantastic tundra tour with stunning views near and far. The forested sections on either end have fast, sharp curves, and the west side has a mellow coast down the Kawuneeche valley (the grade is quite uniform on the steep section). The road's search for scenery also makes it one tough ride. Riding its entire length will keep you above 11,000 feet for 11 miles. Milner Pass is just an afterthought, a spot where the road crosses the Continental Divide. The real summit is not the Continental Divide, but an unnamed high point 24.3 miles west of Estes Park.

EAST TO WEST: Distance from Stanley Village in Estes Park to Community Park in Grand Lake Village: 49 miles

EAST SIDE: Distance from Stanley Village Shopping Center in Estes Park to high point: 24.3 miles

Elevation gain: 4,663 feet

Grades: Maximum 6.8%; average 3% for 11 miles, 5.2% for 10
    miles
Difficulty: 5
WEST SIDE: Distance from Community Park in Grand Lake
    Village to high point: 24.7 miles
Elevation gain: 3,100 feet
Grades: Maximum 5.5%; average 5.3% for 11 miles
Difficulty: 5

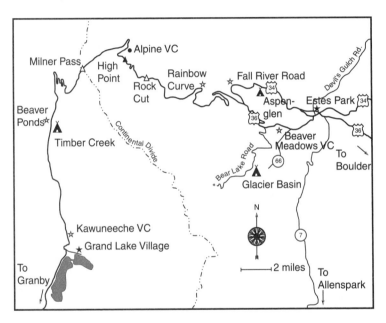

Recommended Start and Stop Points

East Side: Stanley Village (7,520 feet), large shopping
complex on the northeast corner of the intersection of U.S.
Highways 34 and 36 in Estes Park. Stanley Village is easy to
spot, so it's a good spot to meet friends from another city. It
has all the suburban amenities: McDonald's, restaurants, a
coffee shop, a Safeway, movies, pizza, and groceries. There's
plenty of parking too. By starting here, you ride on U.S.
Highway 34, which bypasses the Estes Park tourist district. At

the intersection of U.S. Highways 34 and 36, turn right or use an exit on the west side of the Stanley Village parking lot. You'll pass the Stanley Hotel and continue west on U.S. Highway 34. Note: U.S. Highways 34 and 36 intersect again 8.8 miles west, inside Rocky Mountain National Park.

West Side: Community Park in Grand Lake Village (8,400 feet), 15 miles north of Granby along U.S. Highway 34 on the northern shores of Grand Lake and Shadow Mountain Lake; 24.7 miles and 3,100 feet of elevation gain to the high point. The pleasant, grassy park is surrounded by restaurants, shops, public phones, and groceries.

Alternate Start and Stop Points

East Side: Beaver Meadows Visitors Center (8,200 feet) of Rocky Mountain National Park, on U.S. Highway 36, 4.25 miles west of its junction with U.S. Highway 34 in Estes Park; 19.75 miles and 3,983 feet of elevation gain to the high spot. This spot has water, parking, and rest rooms but little else. Starting here will give you a slightly shorter (by 0.3 mile) route through the

November riding on Trail Ridge Road. Photo by C. Proenza.

lower portion of the national park. Because this alternate start/stop point is a bit off the main route, it isn't included in the mileage log.

Fall River Road trailhead (8,520 feet), on U.S. Highway 36, 7.1 miles west of its junction with U.S. Highway 34 in Estes Park; 17.2 miles and 3,663 feet of elevation gain to the high point. The beginning of this old dirt road is easily seen on a map. You'll save mileage and 1,000 feet of elevation gain, bypass Estes Park, and get to altitude that much sooner. There's picnicking and rest rooms, but during weekends, parking may be tight.

Rainbow Curve (10,820 feet), 16.9 miles west of the intersection of U.S. Highways 34 and 36 in Estes Park; 7.4 miles and 1,363 feet of high-altitude elevation gain to the high point. If you want to avoid all that lowland riding, here's the spot to start. It's got good views too. There are busy rest rooms but no water.

West Side: Kawuneeche Visitors Center (8,700 feet), 2 miles north of Grand Lake Village; 21.7 miles and 2,800 feet of elevation gain to the high point. This is the western twin of Rocky Mountain National Park's Beaver Meadows Visitors Center. As with all visitors centers, you can find water and rest rooms.

Beaver Pond Picnic Area (8,950 feet), 10.3 miles north of Grand Lake Village; 13.3 miles and 3,233 feet of elevation gain to the high point. The Kawuneeche valley is dotted with pleasant spots overlooking the Colorado River; this is just one of them. Beaver Pond and many of the other areas have toilets and picnic tables. From Beaver Pond, the steep curves are only a few miles up the road.

Road and Traffic Conditions

Trail Ridge Road generally has a good, smooth surface, but you can expect some frost-heaves, lumps, and cracked pavement up high. The road on the west side is beautifully maintained, usually clean and smooth. There is rarely a shoulder except for the flat cruise in the Kawuneeche valley on the west side, but the road is wide enough the whole way. The only built-in hazards are drainage grates, which extend beyond the white line, especially below tree line. You can ride over these, but this is best done at low speeds.

The good thing about traffic on this road is that commercial vehicles are prohibited—no trucks! The bad thing is that swarms of drivers are looking at everything but the road. The auto traffic on Trail Ridge Road is horrendous and dangerous. A driver may, at any time, stop dead in the road and fling open a door to photograph a squirrel. However, there is a way to avoid this. Traffic is much better on weekdays. And at the first hint of snow, the Park Service closes the road to autos, but the road is never closed to bicycles. If the road is closed but the weather has been good, chances are you can get your bike up there, especially in early fall.

Descents

West Side and East Side: Sure, you'll want to go screaming down these roads, but that's difficult with all the traffic. Chances are you'll get stuck behind a line of cars. Beware of approaching turnouts and scenic overlooks. There are likely to be people in the road, cars pulling out and in, or cars stopped in the middle of the road.

Sleep and Supplies

There are plenty of restaurants and grocery stores in Estes Park and Grand Lake Village (plus gift shops, public phones, an outdoor clothing store, even a place to rent chainsaws). Nothing, however, is available in the national park except water at visitors' centers or campgrounds during the summer. There is one bike store each in Estes Park, Grand Lake, and Granby, 15 miles south of Grand Lake on U.S. Highway 40. Lodging options in Estes Park range from KOA camping to hotels and riverside cabins. For more information call Estes Park, 800-443-7837, or the Grand Lake Chamber of Commerce, 800-531-1019.

It is always legal to ride a bike on Trail Ridge Road even if it is closed to vehicles. Contact Rocky Mountain National Park, 970-586-1206 or 970-586-1333, for a recording about road and

The west half of Trail Ridge Road.

weather information (the folks on the phones usually have little information on the condition of the road beyond whether it is open or closed), or 970-627-3471 for information on the west side. Dial 911 or 970-586-1399 for emergencies. Park entrance fees are $5 per bike, $15 per car, $30 for an annual pass to RMNP, or $65 for a Golden Eagle pass to all national parks. Save the entry-fee receipt; it's good for a week. If you go past the entrance stations before 7:00 or 8:00 in the morning, they may not be staffed, and you get in free.

Camping in RMNP is on a first-come, first-served basis for all sites except Moraine Park and Glacier Basin. Late May through late September, those sites must be reserved; 800-365-2267. The most useful campsites are Glacier Basin, Aspenglen, and Timber Creek. You can get information for campsites farther afield, from the Forest Service in Estes Park, 970-586-3440, or in Granby, 970-887-4100.

MILEAGE LOG

★0.0 Stanley Village (7,520 feet), at the intersection of U.S. Highways 34 and 36 and Colorado Highway 7, in Estes Park. Movies, McDonald's, pizza, coffee, groceries. Plenty of parking too. To get onto Highway 34, turn right at the intersection of Highways 34 and 36, or use an exit on the west side of the parking lot. You'll pass the Stanley Hotel and continue west on Highway 34.

0.5 Junction with Devil's Gulch Road/County Road 43; continue straight. (To the right, CR 43 will take you 15 miles to Drake; this is a great side trip with little traffic and steep switchbacks.)

4.7 Soda and Pop Stop on the left. With the exception of the visitors' centers in RMNP, there's no place to get water in the park, so this is your last chance if you've forgotten anything.

5.0 Fall River Entrance Station (8,240 feet).

6.4 Horseshoe Park. A good place to see elk. Traffic here is often clogged and confused.

☆7.1 Fall River Road (8,520 feet) on the right. Picnic tables, rest rooms, sufficient parking on weekdays.

8.8 T-junction with U.S. Highway 36; turn right. If you started at the Beaver Meadows Entrance Station, this is where

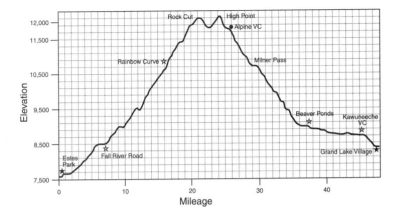

you join the main route. (To the left, Highway 36 goes to the Beaver Meadows Entrance Station, Park Headquarters, and Visitors Center, and back to Estes Park.)

9.3 View of Mount Ypsilon dead ahead.

11.3 Hidden Valley turnoff, 15 mph curve. From here on up, the grade is relentless.

12.8 Many Parks Curve. That huge, flat-topped mountain is Longs Peak.

15.7 Pullout with running stream in spring and summer.

16.3 Sign says "2 miles above sea level, 10,560 ft."

☆16.9 Rainbow Curve (10,820 feet). Good views, toilets, parking. When the Park Service closes the road, this is usually the gate it locks. If the weather's good and the road looks ridable, hop the gate and get it all to yourself!

18.8 Scenic overlook. Good views of Meeker, Longs, Pagoda, and Notchtop Peaks.

19.8 Forest Canyon Overlook.

21.3 Rock Cut. Pedestrian walkways, parking, toilets. Slow to 15 miles per hour—there is often a crowd wandering around here. It's a good place to stop, but not quite the high point.

22.9 Iceberg Pass (11,824 feet). This is the low point between the Rock Cut and the High Point.

▲24.3 High Point (12,183 feet).

25.9 Alpine Visitors Center. During the summer, you can get water here and see Park Service displays about tundra.

26.4 Wicked curve.

30.2 Milner Pass (10,759 feet).

32.4 Fairview curve; begin a series of 15 mph curves.

36.4 Grade ends.

☆37.6 Beaver Pond Picnic Area (8,950 feet) on the right. Picnic tables, trash receptacles, parking, rest rooms.

38.1 Timber Creek Campground.

46.0 Grand Lake Entrance Station.

☆46.6 Kawuneeche Visitors Center (8,700 feet) on the left. Parking, displays, rangers to answer questions.

47.9 Turnoff for Grand Lake Village on the left just before a gas station.

★49.0 Community Park (8,400 feet), in the center of Grand Lake Village. The pleasant, grassy park is surrounded by more things than you'll need: restaurants, gift shops, public phones, an outdoor clothing store, groceries, even a place to rent chainsaws.

4   WILLOW CREEK PASS
9,620 feet

Generally, a road is most spectacular and fun near the top. Not so with Willow Creek Pass. Here, the lower portions of the road steal the show. To the north, there are the typically steep last few miles to the top, but south of this the road bobs through the forest like a roller coaster. Going up or down, your derailleurs will get a workout. The southern side, although it gains a respectable 1,700 feet, is primarily a low-angle cruise through aspens and along a winding creek choked with, you guessed it, willows. This is a great autumn ride for anyone who likes colors without traffic. This pass is described from south to north because the south side is longer and closer to urban areas and major highways.

SOUTH TO NORTH: Distance from Windy Gap Viewing Area
to Rand: 31.6 miles
SOUTH SIDE: Distance from Windy Gap Viewing Area to
Willow Creek Pass: 21.8 miles
Elevation gain: 1,769 feet
Grades: Maximum 5%; average 1.1% for 15.7 miles, 3.8% for
3.1 miles, 4.6% for 2.1 miles, 5.0% for 1 mile
Difficulty: 2
NORTH SIDE: Distance from Rand to Willow Creek Pass: 9.8
miles
Elevation gain: 996 feet
Grades: Maximum 5.3%; average 1.3% for 3.7 miles, 4.3% for
2 miles, 5.3% for 3.7 miles
Difficulty: 1

Recommended Start and Stop Points

South Side: Windy Gap Viewing Area (7,851 feet), at the
intersection of U.S. Highway 40 and Colorado Highway 125,
2 miles west of Granby; 21.7 miles and 1,769 feet of elevation
gain to Willow Creek Pass. This rest area seems to have been
built expressly for riding Willow Creek Pass. It sports a half
dozen wind-sheltered picnic tables and a few rest rooms.

North Side: Rand (8,600 feet), at the junction of Colorado
Highway 125 and Jackson County Road 27; 9.4 miles and just
under 1,000 feet of elevation gain to Willow Creek Pass. Rand is
a few buildings and several haystacks; a general store here is not
always open. Across the street from the store is a parking area
posted "No Overnight Parking." The best parking area is the
widest, unoccupied pullout.

Alternate Start and Stop Points

South Side: City Park (7,830 feet) a few blocks north of Main
Street on Zero Street in Granby; 24.5 miles and 1,790 feet of elevation gain to Willow Creek Pass. This park is well signed,
located behind tennis courts and next to the Granby Chamber
of Commerce building, if you'd like to start in Granby.

Pullout (8,360 feet) on the right on Colorado Highway 125 at

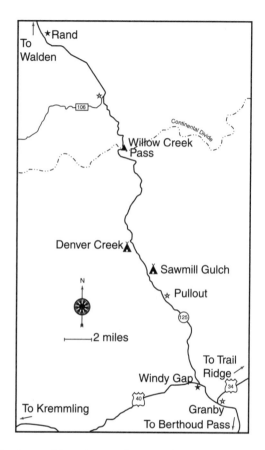

mile 7.8; about 14 miles and 1,260 feet of elevation gain to Willow Creek Pass. This will cut out the up and down of the initial section without sacrificing much elevation, but it is only a pullout and has no facilities.

Denver Creek Campground (8,640 feet) on the left on Colorado Highway 125 at mile 12.5; 9.25 miles and 980 feet of elevation gain to Willow Creek Pass. This is a good place to start if you'd like an out-and-back to Rand. This is also the most extensive campsite in the canyon. (The Sawmill Gulch Campground 2 miles south of Denver Creek is also an option.)

North Side: Intersection of Colorado Highway 125 and Forest Road 106 (8,876 feet), 4.4 miles south of Rand; 5 miles and 744 feet of elevation gain to Willow Creek Pass. This is a large signed area with plenty of room to park, but no other facilities. Starting here will cut the northern side in half while still letting you ride the most interesting parts of the road.

Road and Traffic Conditions

Willow Creek doesn't have a shoulder or traffic. The road can be rough, especially at the intersections of ranch or Forest Service roads. Near the top, the road goes through some debris-shedding rock cuts. There are no wrenching hairpins and visibility is good, so if a truck brushes within inches, at least you'll know it wasn't accidental.

Descents

South Side: No place for speed records. The turns won't slow you down, but at times it feels as though the grade won't speed you up.

North Side: The real jewel. After a steady drop for 2 miles, 3 miles of steep up and down will make you work to keep the momentum up. It's like interval training on a beautiful, lonely road.

Sleep and Supplies

Food is available in Granby and sometimes at the general store in Rand, which may or may not be open. Water is available at Denver Creek and Stillwater Campgrounds. Granby has everything a cyclist might need, including a bike shop, Great Divide Sports—primarily a mountain bike rental shop, but they do have tubes, tires, and odds and ends for road bikes—and even a good mechanic. When riding the north side, you're pretty much on your own; there are no public facilities beyond Rand until Walden, 22 miles to the north. For more information, call the Greater Granby Chamber of Commerce, 970-887-2311, on the south; to the north, contact the North Park Chamber of Commerce, 970-723-4600.

For information about camping contact the Sulphur Ranger District in Granby, 970-887-4100, or the Arapaho Roosevelt

National Forest, 970-498-2770. There are no camping restrictions along Colorado Highway 125, but there is a fair amount of private property. Established campgrounds are at Sawmill Gulch and Denver Creek.

MILEAGE LOG

★0   Windy Gap Viewing Area (7,851 feet) at the intersection of U.S. Highway 40 and Colorado Highway 125. An elaborate, well signed, fully equipped rest area next to a municipal power station.

3.7 Pass the C Lazy U Ranch.

5.1 Shadow M Ranch; good aspens.

☆7.8 Large pullout (8,360 feet) on the left. A good place to start for shaving some mileage and the initial hill.

10.4 Sawmill Gulch Campground. There is water here.

☆12.5 Denver Creek Campground (8,640 feet) on the left. Water also available here; Denver Creek is more extensive than Sawmill Gulch.

17.0 Stillwater Pass turnoff/Forest Road 107 on the right. Meandering Stillwater Creek meets Willow Creek here.

18.6 Parkview Mountain comes into view.

19.9 Sign says "Willow Creek Pass Summit 2 miles."

▲21.8 Willow Creek Pass (9,620 feet). Large shoulder on either side of the road, but this doesn't last long. No facilities here, and the sign doesn't bother to mention the elevation.

24.3 Good view here. The road goes straight through a rock cut, and then shoots up the first of a series of small hills.

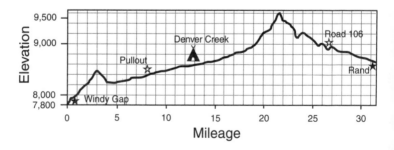

25.2 The road goes through a series of curves while going over small hills.

☆26.6 Forest Road 106 (8,876 feet) on the left. No facilities here, just plenty of room to park near the large intersection. This is the best alternate start for the north side of Willow Pass.

27.3 The road gets really straight and the grade eases. You are leaving the mountains and entering North Park.

29.6 Old Homestead Lodge and RV cabins on the right.

30.0 Out of the trees and onto the plain.

★31.6 Rand (8,620 feet), at Jackson County Road 27 (which connects with Colorado Highway 14 near Gould). Immediately before this road is a turnoff area that is large enough to park in. Across the street from the general store is a long pullout area posted "No Overnight Parking."

5   GORE PASS
9,527 feet

Gore Pass is as much a plateau ride as a mountain ride. Like Rabbit Ears Pass (ride 2), it has a west summit in addition to the main pass. Between the two high points are 9 miles of rolling hills and steep steps. The riding is enjoyable, but all the up and down makes the miles between the summits seem pretty long. There are few services near Gore Pass, and on the east side all but the last 2 miles are across private land. Colorado Highway 134 is lonely and beautiful but without extremes.

EAST TO WEST: Distance from Kremmling Town Park to Tonopas General Store: 33.8 miles
EAST SIDE: Distance from junction of Highways 40 and 134 to summit: 11 miles
Elevation gain: 1,967 feet

Grades: Maximum 6.8%; average 1.6% for 3.5 miles, 4.0% for
   4.6 miles, 5.6% for 2.5 miles
Difficulty: 2
WEST SIDE: Distance from Tonopas General Store to summit:
   16.7 miles
Elevation gain: 1,244 feet; 360 feet must be gained twice
Grades: Maximum 7.0%; average 0.5% for 8 miles, 3.2% for 1.9
   miles, 4.4% for 2.8 miles, 5.8% for 2.4 miles
Difficulty: 2

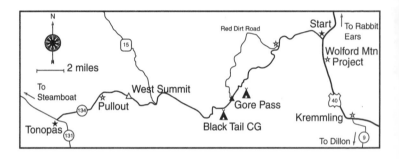

Recommended Start and Stop Points

East Side: Junction of U.S. Highway 40 and Colorado
Highway 134 (7,557 feet), 6.1 miles west of Kremmling Town
Park; 11 miles and 1,970 feet elevation gain to Gore Pass. At this
wide spot on two roads, there is nothing but gravel and sun.
The heat will die down in the trees, especially in the afternoon.
Drive up Highway 134 a bit to get away from the roar of traffic
on U.S. 40. Riding to the west summit and back is a good
40-mile ride.

West Side: Tonopas General Store (8,280 feet), near the
junction of Highways 134 and 131; 16.7 miles and 1,244 feet
of elevation gain to Gore Pass. This is a wide spot with a store,
but it is a real general store in the sense that you can buy a bit
of anything here. Start anywhere near here; there is also a
spacious pullout 1.4 miles west of Tonopas.

Alternate Start and Stop Points

East Side: Kremmling Town Park (7,360 feet), in the center of Kremmling on Park Street/U.S. Highway 40 and Third; 17.1 miles and 2,167 feet elevation gain to Gore Pass. If you'd like to start and finish in pleasant surroundings, Kremmling Town Park is the place. This patch of green has sprouted picnic tables, rest rooms, public telephones, and grass for stretching on. It is surrounded by supermarkets, restaurants, bars, ATMs, and liquor stores. Coffee shops and hotels are also within eyeshot.

Wolford Mountain Project (7,500 feet), on U.S. Highway 40, 4.4 miles north of Kremmling; 12.7 miles and 2,027 feet of elevation gain to Gore Pass. The Wolford Mountain Project and the Wolford Mountain Reservoir are on BLM land, but the recreational facilities are managed by a concessionaire. It costs three dollars to park and use a picnic table.

Red Dirt Road 100 (7,840 feet), on the right on Highway 134, 4 miles west of U.S. Highway 40; 7 miles and 1,687 feet of elevation gain to Gore Pass. This is a well-signed road on the north side of the canyon. There is room to park here but nothing else. All the surrounding land is private until 2 miles below Gore Pass. Riding from here will put you on the steep grade right away.

West Side: Pullout (8,400 feet) on the south side of Highway 134, 4.2 miles east of Tonopas; 12.5 miles and 1,127 feet of elevation gain to Gore Pass. To skip the flats outside of Tonopas, start from this pullout.

West Summit (9,040 feet), on Highway 134, 7.2 miles east of Tonopas; 9.6 miles and 487 feet of elevation gain to Gore Pass. There is a gated road to the right and enough space to pull off the highway. The West Summit is a good place to start on a hot day. This option cuts the distance in half.

Road and Traffic Conditions

U.S. Highway 40 is best ridden in the morning; by noon it's as much fun as an Arizona interstate. Colorado Highway 134 is quiet. Traffic peaks during hunting season, but otherwise there are local ranch trucks and an occasional tourist. It is a small road with a small shoulder, but curves aren't especially tight, and good visibility gives people plenty of space to pass. Public land extends only 2 miles east of Gore Pass; east of that, many small ranch roads and driveways fan gravel onto the highway. The section between the two summits is rough in places, with an occasional jarring pothole and plenty of cattle guards.

Descents

West Side: You'll do a remarkable amount of climbing to get down. The few steep sections are brief, and the effort needed to make it over the west summit can be disheartening if you've powered up Gore Pass from the east. The final descent into Tonopas is surprisingly straight.

East Side: This is pleasant but without extremes. Straightaways alternate with series of 25 to 40 mph curves as you drop from high, rolling hills into rangeland and creek-cut flats.

Sleep and Supplies

The eastern side of Gore Pass is hot and dry below 8,000 feet. Kremmling has more restaurants than you might expect; to the west, there is only the Tonopas General Store, where you can get gas and an immense variety of packaged food, and the nearest restaurant is in Yampa or Oak Creek, to the south on Colorado Highway 9. The only potable water along Highway 134 is at Gore Pass and Blacktail Campgrounds. Bike stores are in Steamboat Springs to the north and in Granby to the east, both on U.S. Highway 40. For information on the east side, contact the Kremmling Chamber, 970-724-3472; on the west side contact Steamboat Springs, 970-879-0882.

All the land around the start and stop points is private. The land on the summit is administered by Routt National Forest, 970-879-1870. The only two campsites, Gore Pass and Blacktail Campgrounds, are part of the Kremmling Ranger District, 970-724-9004.

MILEAGE LOG

☆0   Kremmling Town Park (7,360 feet), on Park Street and Third. Picnic tables, rest rooms, public phones.

☆4.4 Wolford Mountain Project (7,500 feet). Public land managed by a concessionaire—you must pay $3 to drive in; picnic spots, water.

★6.1 Junction with Colorado Highway 134 (7,557 feet); turn onto Highway 134.

☆10.2 Red Dirt Road 100 (7,840 feet) on the right side of Highway 134.

16.9 Huge pullout on the right.

▲17.1 Gore Pass (9,527 feet). Large summit area with typical pulloffs. Campground right on the top of the pass is a good place to get water.

18.6 Blacktail Creek Campground. This pleasant campsite has water.

18.8 Blacktail Creek Picnic Area. Rest rooms, picnic tables, parking.

21.5 Roads 100 and 250.

22.5 Pullout on the left; leaving Grand County.

24.6 Rock Creek area. Forest Road 206 heads to the south and Routt County Road 15 leads north to Lake Lagunita and Lynx Pass.

☆26.5 West Summit of Gore Pass (9,040 feet); pullout on the left.

☆29.6 Pullout on the south (8,400 feet). This is a good place

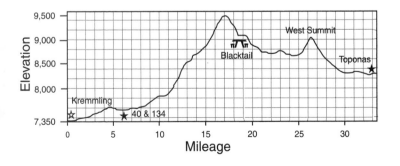

to start from the west side if you want to skip Tonopas and the flats just outside of town.

33.1 Cross railroad track.

33.3 Junction with Colorado Highway 131; stay on Highway 134.

★33.8 Tonopas General Store (8,280 feet). This small store sells just about everything. There are no other facilities, so to start from here you must park along the road.

CENTRAL COLORADO

6 BERTHOUD PASS
11,315 feet

Berthoud Pass is perfect in a lot of ways. It's easy to get to, it's scenic and winding, and it has excellent facilities on both sides for either a day trip or a tour. Some of these strengths, however, are also its undoing. U.S. Highway 40 hosts a horde of recreational traffic and a fair amount of commercial traffic. The south side of the pass is really too narrow to support all this traffic as well as bikes. Hopefully this will change after the construction, but that won't be until after 2006. The north side is nothing but fun. The road is big enough for everyone, allowing you to sweep into Winter Park with liberating speed.

SOUTH TO NORTH: Distance from Easter Seals Handi-Camp lot to Hideaway Park: 27.5 miles

SOUTH SIDE: Distance from Arapaho National Forest sign to Berthoud Pass: 11 miles

Elevation gain: 2,527 feet

Grades: Maximum 5.5%; average 2.1% for 2.1 miles, 4.8% for 6.5 miles, 5.2% for 3.8 miles

Difficulty: 3

NORTH SIDE: Distance from Midland Picnic Area to Berthoud Pass: 8.8 miles

Elevation gain: 1,915 feet

Grades: Maximum 5.0%; 2.5% for 6.4 miles, 4.6% for 6.9 miles

Difficulty: 2

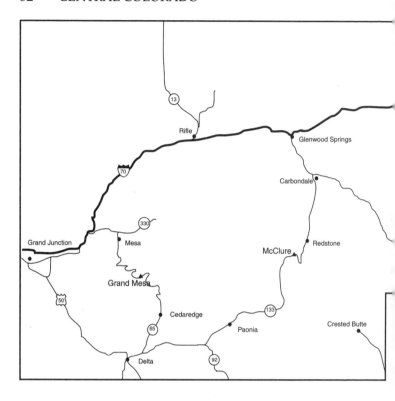

Recommended Start and Stop Points

South Side: Arapaho National Forest sign (8,788 feet) on the north side of U.S. Highway 40, 3.3 miles from its junction with Interstate 70; 11 miles and 2,527 feet of elevation gain to Berthoud Pass. Granted, a sign is an odd place to recommend as a starting point, but it is easy to find and hassle free if you don't want to park in Empire. There is shady space here for a few cars.

North Side: Midland Picnic Area (9,400 feet) on U.S. Highway 40, 0.5 mile west of Mary Jane Ski Area (mileage and altitude change to top, 8.8 miles and 1,915 feet of elevation gain to Berthoud Pass). This idyllic spot is far enough off the highway to be quiet and out of sight—which makes it easy to miss, but it is just behind a green Winter Park City Limit sign. There

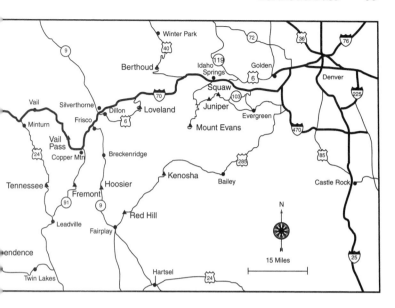

are picnic tables, rest rooms, and dark mushroom-full woods. There is no water, unfortunately.

Alternate Start and Stop Points

South Side: Easter Seals Handi-Camp parking lot (8,261 feet), at the intersection of exit 233 off Interstate 70 and the frontage road; 14.3 miles and 3,054 feet of elevation gain to Berthoud Pass. The generous parking area is marked by an Easter Seals sign. This is a good place to start to maximize the climbing, but the area is somewhat grungy.

Clear Creek Picnic Area (9,456 feet) on the left on U.S. Highway 40, 6 miles west of I-70; 8.3 miles and 1,859 feet of elevation gain to Berthoud Pass. A large sign on the south side of the road marks this great area; it's big with lots of shade near

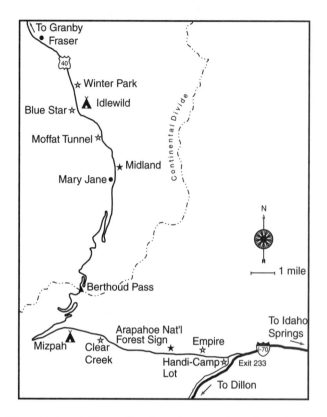

the West Fork of Clear Creek. It has no fees, but there is no water. It's a great place to start if you don't mind giving up some distance and elevation gain.

North Side: Hideaway Park and Winter Park Visitors Center (8,807 feet) in central Winter Park, at Highway 40 and East Mid-Town Road; 13.2 miles and 2,508 feet of elevation gain to Berthoud Pass. This park is not hidden away; it is dead in the center of Winter Park, close to everything. This is the best spot if you'd like to start or stop near food and beer. It adds 50 percent more distance to the Midland Picnic Area recommended start/stop.

Idlewild Campground/Blue Starr Picnic Area (8,948 feet) on U.S. Highway 40, 1 mile south of downtown Winter Park; 11.9 miles and 2,367 feet of elevation gain to Berthoud Pass.

Starting down Berthoud Pass. Photo by C. Proenza.

Idlewild Campground is on the right (east) side of the road and Blue Starr Picnic Area is just across the road—it's not as easy to see as Idlewild, but it is there. This spot has toilets and picnic tables, but it is not as pleasant as Midland.

Road and Traffic Conditions

If traffic bothers you at all, stay away from the south side of Berthoud Pass, or ride on a weekday morning. It's that bad, and until the construction is over, the road is a tour de jersey barriers anyway. The construction has made many scrapes and divots in the road, and unless the road is completely resurfaced, these are jarring. The north side, however, is fantastic. There's still a lot of traffic, but the road is plenty big enough for you and all your behemoth neighbors. Because this is such a heavily used road in winter, the highway department spreads a ton of sand and gravel, and this stuff never completely washes away.

Descents

South Side: The road is such that it's nearly impossible not to mix with traffic and use the whole lane. The last 8 miles into Empire are straight and a great place to catch a tailwind.

North Side: The north side of Berthoud is not too fast; the long switchbacks keep the grade down, and as soon as you start picking up real speed, you're faced with a 20 mph curve. Large shoulders for bikes and more lanes for traffic are much better than the south side.

Sleep and Supplies

Berthoud Pass is the place to travel light. There are plenty of opportunities for food and water around, and they are so conveniently spaced that forgetting the water bottle is no big deal. There is a small cafeteria on the pass itself, with sodas, sandwiches, vending machines, and rest rooms. Winter Park and Empire are towns geared to serve, and there is also water at the Forest Service campgrounds. The nearest bike parts are to be found in Winter Park. It is a mountain biking town, so despite its size and several bike stores, you'll still find that for road bikes there's little more than tires, tubes, and tools. Lodging is not a problem because the ski areas are always eager for summer visitors. For more information, contact the Winter Park–Fraser Valley Chamber of Commerce, 970-887-9235.

Berthoud Pass is in Arapaho Roosevelt National Forest, 970-498-2770. The south side is within the Clear Creek Ranger District, 303-567-3000; the north side is run by the Sulphur Ranger District, 970-887-4100. Dispersed camping is difficult along U.S. Highway 40 because much of the land along it is either owned or effectively owned by mining interests or ski areas. There is plenty of excellent established camping on both sides, but the fees are steep, usually $10. Mizpah Campground is on the south side; Idlewild Campground, on the north side, has a campground host. Because the campsites are close to towns, it is easy to travel light but eat heavy.

MILEAGE LOG

☆0   Easter Seal Handi-Camp lot (8,261 feet) at exit 233 off I-70. Look for boulders, abandoned cars, and an Easter Seals sign. Follow U.S. Highway 40 west.

1.0 Coming into the town of Empire.

1.3 Intersection with North Empire/Bard Street in Empire.

2.8 Mountain Meadow Camp.

3.1 Italian restaurant on the left.

★3.3 Arapaho National Forest sign (8,788 feet) on the right. Small pullout behind the sign.

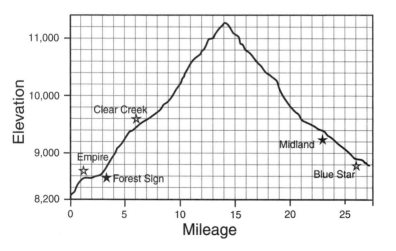

3.5 Two lanes going up (west) and one lane going down (east). The road is so heavily sanded during the winter that it is never completely sand-free.

3.9 Large pullout.

4.8 Huge pullout and a 50 mph curve.

5.2 The road is rough to good, the shoulder excellent when gravel free.

6.0 Clear Creek Picnic Area on the left. Lots of shade, no fees, no water.

7.3 Mizpah Campground; good camping.

8.2 Berthoud Falls. A grocery with snacks.

8.5 Road for the Henderson mine.

8.8 The first of many curves. From here the road is tight; there is little shoulder. This should improve after the construction, but as of 2001, it's a mess.

9.5 Roadwork begins here.

10.2 Extra lane ends; 20 mph curve and tons of traffic.

▲ 14.3 Berthoud Pass (11,315 feet) and top of the Continental Divide. The Berthoud Pass Ski Area offers scenic chairlift rides during the summer, so some of the concessions are open. You can get soda or sandwiches in a small cafeteria.

14.6 Pullout. The road north of the top is rough and broken.

14.9 The north side of Berthoud is much better than the south, which is apparent as soon as you hit this section of 20 mph curves. There is a good shoulder and enough lanes to keep traffic from piling up behind slow-moving vehicles.

19.7 The road surface is new, but there is no shoulder. Instead, there is a gutter full of rocks and debris.

22.4 Fishing hole and pullout.

22.6 Mary Jane Ski Area.

★ 23.1 Midland Picnic Area (9,400 feet) on the right. This is the best starting point for the north side of the pass. A couple of picnic tables, rest rooms, a scenic dumpster, no water.

24.5 Winter Park Ski Area. Hotels, parking, everything.

24.8 Moffat Tunnel Overlook (9,044 feet) directly above the train tunnel. Mostly overlooks the skier parking lot; many informative plaques. Not a bad alternate start.

☆26.2 Idlewild Campground on the right, Blue Starr Picnic Area on the left (8,948 feet). The picnic area is much harder to see but is right across the road. Toilets, tables. This area is not as secluded or pleasant as Midland.

27.2 Downtown Winter Park. Everything you might want is here, though mountain bikes rule the town.

☆27.5 Hideaway Park and Winter Park Visitors Center (8,807 feet) at the corner of U.S. Highway 40 and East Mid-Town Road. This is the best spot if you'd like to start or stop near food and beer.

7   SQUAW and JUNIPER PASSES
11,130 feet (High Point)

The Squaw Pass road is small and winding at the bottom near Interstate 70, but it opens up as you go higher. There are good views to the north, and during autumn the road is speckled with gold aspen leaves. Colorado Highway 103 is not much of a road and has very little shoulder, but there is a lot of traffic, especially on the lower portions, which serve residential areas. Most maps show this pass as Squaw Pass, and some may show Juniper Pass, but as with Trail Ridge Road (ride 3), you are not really riding over these passes. The road goes from east to west over a long ridge line, and both Squaw and Juniper Passes are north-south passes. You travel perpendicular to them instead of up and over them. This should be called the Warrior Mountain Road because the road nearly goes over the top of Warrior Mountain on its way to Echo Lake. Although this ride can be combined with the Mount Evans ascent (ride 8)—it is an excellent way to ride to Mount Evans—the Squaw and Juniper Passes ride is fun enough and big enough to be a ride in itself.

EAST TO WEST: Distance from Fillius Park to Echo Lake: 18.7 miles

EAST SIDE: Distance from Fillius Park to high point: 16 miles
Elevation gain: 3,353 feet
Grades: Maximum 11%; average 4.2% for 1.6 miles, 5% for 22
    miles
Difficulty: 4
WEST SIDE: Distance from Echo Lake to high point: 2.7 miles
Elevation gain: 470 feet
Grades: Maximum 4.2%; average 3.6% for 1 mile, 4.2% for 1.1
    miles
Difficulty: 1

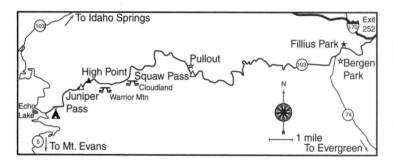

Recommended Start and Stop Points

East Side: Fillius Park (7,777 feet) near Bergen Park just to
the right (north) of the intersection of Colorado Highway 74
and Bergen Parkway; 16 miles and 3,353 feet of elevation gain to
the high point. From Interstate 70, take the El Rancho exit/exit
252 and follow Colorado Highway 74 west. Fillius Park is a
well-built Denver Mountain park open from 5:00 A.M. to 11:00
P.M. Look for the stone gazebos and picnic tables. There are
rest rooms in the middle of the park, plenty of shade trees and
parking, but no water.

West Side: Echo Lake area (10,660 feet) at the intersection of
Colorado Highways 5 and 103; 2.7 miles and 470 feet of elevation gain to the high point. You can park outside the fee station,
near the gift store, or at lakeside picnic areas 0.5 mile north on
Highway 103.

Alternate Start and Stop Points

East Side: RTD (Regional Transportation District) Park and Ride at Interstate 70 and El Rancho, immediately off exit 252, 1.8 miles east of Fillius Park; 16 miles and 3,353 feet of elevation gain to the high point. There are no other facilities here, but there are restaurants and gas stations nearby. Because it is so easy to spot, this makes a good rendezvous point and adds 1.8 miles and no appreciable elevation.

Arapaho National Forest sign and pullout (9,797 feet) on the right on Highway 103, 10.1 miles west of Fillius Park; 6 miles and 1,333 feet of elevation gain to the high point. This cuts out the busiest, narrowest portion of the road to the east and can still provide a lot of riding for anyone going higher on the Mount Evans road. There is space here for a couple of cars on an otherwise narrow road.

Road and Traffic Conditions

Colorado Highway 103 is a charming rural road for its lower 10 miles from Colorado Highway 74 west. Unfortunately, a lot of people use it, and because the road is small and tightly curved with a minimal shoulder, expect cars to pass closely. After 10 miles, the residential traffic dies out and there are only a few tourists. The pavement is good most of the way, and the top has good shoulders.

Descents

East Side: This road is so curved and twisted that your bike will be rocking from side to side the whole way down. It's hard to go full out for long because of other vehicles on the road. Beware cars swinging out into the oncoming lane while passing bicyclists.

West Side: This side is not fast or long but beware of Echo Lake traffic as you hit the bottom of the hill.

Sleep and Supplies

Most of this ride is in Clear Creek County, but the towns near the start are in Jefferson County. For information, call the Evergreen Area Chamber of Commerce, 303-674-3412.

This area is in Arapaho Roosevelt National Forest, 970-498-2770, the Clear Creek Ranger District, 303-567-3000. The only camping along this road is near Echo Lake, where Highway 103 meets Highway 5 (Mount Evans Road). Although, because this area is so close to Denver, it's not that necessary to camp. Echo Lake is right on the highway.

MILEAGE LOG

★0   Fillius Park (7,777 feet) near Bergen Park just to the right (north) of the intersection of Colorado Highway 74 east and Bergen Parkway. Stone gazebo, picnic tables, rest rooms, grills, plenty of shade trees and parking; no water.

0.1 Intersection with Colorado Highway 74 east; turn right and ride a mile to get to 74 and 103, which is the center of Bergen Park.

1.1 Junction with Colorado Highway 103; turn right. This is a busy, mall-dominated intersection. Just downhill are some athletic fields that have plenty of parking, but during the

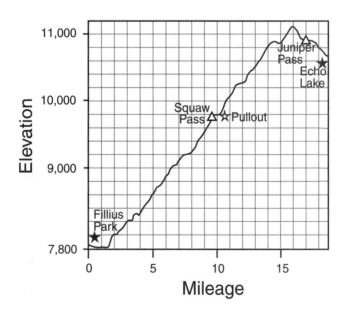

summer may swell to overflowing during softball, soccer, or Little League events. As you start up Highway 103, there is a sign for "Mount Evans fee station, 18 miles" and the first of several "share the road" signs blotted out with red paint.

6.9 Intersection with Sinton Hill Road.

7.3 Pullout on the right.

7.4 Another pullout, this one with a small meadow and aspens.

8.1 Poor pavement.

9.3 Pullout.

9.6 Squaw Pass (8,970 feet), at intersection with Bear Creek Road. Great views down the valley and the road improves, but there's still no shoulder.

9.9 Pullout on the right.

☆10.1 Arapaho National Forest sign and large pullout (9,797 feet) on the right. No suitable camping here.

13.3 Large pullout on the right.

14.8 Cloud Land Picnic Area. Picnic tables and rest rooms in a pretty area. From here to Juniper Pass, there is a picnic area about every 2 miles. There is no water at picnic areas along the way but plenty at Echo Lake.

15.7 Scenic overlook.

15.9 Warrior Mountain Picnic Area. Picnic tables and rest rooms.

▲16.0 High point (11,130 feet). There is some downhill, but not much.

16.3 Eagle's Aerie Picnic Area. The upper part of the Mount Evans road comes into view.

16.8 Juniper Pass Picnic Area.

17.0 Pullouts at Juniper Pass (10,906 feet). Unmarked and unnoticeable, Juniper Pass is not as spectacular as many of the overlooks along the way.

17.3 Large pullouts on the left; excellent views.

★18.7 Echo Lake complex (10,660 feet) at intersection with Colorado Highway 5, the Mount Evans Road.

8   MOUNT EVANS
14,150 feet

Mount Evans is big, really big. From Idaho Springs at Interstate 70 to the top is a full 1.25 miles of vertical gain. Besides the constant climbing, what really makes riding Mount Evans unique is the altitude. Climbing from 12,000 to 14,000 feet is a lot different from climbing from 10,000 to 12,000 feet. Wind is another difficulty. Above tree line, the wind gets a clean shot, and because the road switchbacks so wildly, no matter which way the wind is blowing and no matter which way you are going, you'll be faced with head winds on a steep road. The

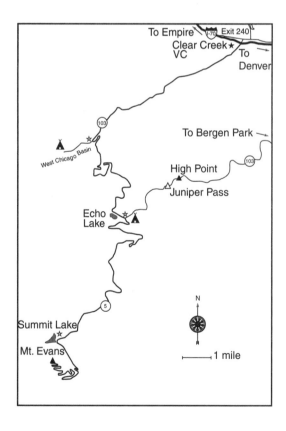

climb is not constantly steep, however. There are breaks at Echo Lake and even a slight downhill before Summit Lake, but mostly this is the place to push hard and breath harder. Because this is a mountaintop, not a pass, this ride is described just as an out-and-back.

EAST SIDE: Distance from Idaho Springs to summit of Mount Evans: 28.2 miles
Elevation gain: 6,610 feet
Grades: Maximum 10% to Echo Lake; average 3% for 3.3 miles, 4.3% for 3.4 miles, 5.8% for 5.8 miles; from Echo Lake to summit, average 5.6% for 5.5 miles, 4.1%for 2.7 miles, 5.8% for 1.25 miles, 5.6% for 3 miles
Difficulty: 5

Recommended Start and Stop Point

East Side: Clear Creek Ranger Station and Visitors Center (7,540 feet) in Idaho Springs; 28.2 miles and 6,610 feet of elevation gain to Mount Evans. From Interstate 70, take exit 240 at the signs for Mount Evans and go south just across the bridge over the interstate to the large Forest Service Information Center. There is ample parking here, and you can water up, look at displays about the Mount Evans area, or shop for Colorado books. The center is open 8:00 A.M. to 5:00 P.M. daily except holidays.

Alternate Start and Stop Points

East Side: Fillius Park (7,775 feet) in Bergen Park—see ride 7, Squaw and Juniper Passes; 33.9 miles and 6,375 feet of elevation gain to Mount Evans. It's just as easy, in fact easier, to skip the drive to Idaho Springs and instead ride to Mount Evans via Squaw Pass. The ride from Fillius Park is 5.7 miles longer but 240 vertical feet shorter. If you'd like to tack on a few more miles and still get a high start, pick one of the several picnic areas on Colorado Highway 103 just east of Echo Lake (see ride 7, Squaw and Juniper Passes).

West Chicago Creek (8,842 feet) on Colorado Highway 103,

6.4 miles southwest of the ranger station; 21.8 miles and 5,308 feet of elevation gain to Mount Evans. Where Highway 103 takes a sharp turn and leaves the valley, a dirt road continues along Chicago Creek to the West Chicago Creek Campground. Right at the intersection of these roads, there is enough space to park. There are more pleasant spots close by, but starting from here shaves the warm-up miles and still leaves all the steep climbing. The summit is still a mile straight up.

Echo Lake area (10,660 feet) at the intersection of Colorado Highways 5 and 103; 15.2 miles and 3,481 feet of elevation gain to Mount Evans. You can park outside the fee station, near the gift store, or at lakeside picnic areas 0.5 mile north on Highway 103. It's $3 per person per bike (sorry, no break for tandems) to ascend Mount Evans. The fee station is unstaffed after the road is closed for the winter. The toughest miles start from here, and a bit more than half the elevation gain lies above.

Summit Lake (12,840 feet) on Colorado Highway 5; 5.9 miles and 1,315 feet of elevation gain to Mount Evans. This is a great way to ride the most unique part of this road without the entire grind. Summit Lake is well above tree line. There is parking here, and a lot of people mill around. This is also a good place to start if someone volunteers to drive down to Idaho Springs so the rest of the group can ride down.

Road and Traffic Conditions

The road northwest up to Echo Lake is pretty good. Granted, the shoulder sometimes is narrow and sports gravel, but the surface is smooth and uncracked, and the road is wide enough for bikes and cars. Because this is almost exclusively a scenic road, trucks are rare. Above Echo Lake, and especially above Summit Lake, the road is like plastic; it is sometimes warped and heaved, but is usually smooth. There is no shoulder to speak of, which isn't so bad because it can take a lot of lane to dodge rocks or the occasional hat-sized hole. Above Summit Lake, weekend traffic can be extremely slow because people are gawking as much as driving, which is understandable. This is not as much of a problem going up, but it's a pity to be stuck behind a row of brake lights on a road that throws bikes downhill. Fortunately, this road is almost always ridable in autumn after it has been closed to cars. It is colder, to be sure, but afternoon thunderstorms aren't as bad, and a bit of water and ice on the road is much better to deal with than strings of cars. It can also be ridable when still closed in spring, but is more likely to have occasional snowdrifts.

Descent

The upper part, from the summit to Summit Lake, can be frustrating and take some work. The road is steep, but it's not possible to go very fast through one 10 mph curve after another. On a windy day, you may feel as though you're going up and down instead of just down. There is a short climb after Summit Lake, and after that the real speed begins. The grade mellows about 6 miles from Idaho Springs, but this still leaves about 15 miles of blurred scenery.

Sleep and Supplies

Food and beverages are readily available in Idaho Springs. For more information, call the Clear Creek County Tourism Board, 800-882-5278 or 303-567-4660.

Mount Evans is in Arapaho Roosevelt National Forest, 970-498-2770, the Clear Creek Ranger District, 303-567-3000. There is actually some camping along Highways 103 and 5, although because this area is so close to Denver, it's not that necessary to camp. Even so, there are two usable campsites, West Chicago Creek and Echo Lake. West Chicago Creek Campground is a few miles down a dirt road west of the highway; Echo Lake is right on the highway. There is a restaurant and gift shop at Echo Lake, but no other water along the road.

MILEAGE LOG

★0.0 Clear Creek Ranger Station and Visitors Center (7,540 feet), at exit 240 off I-70. Rest rooms, water available 8:00 A.M.–5:00 P.M. daily excluding holidays.

3.7 Trout Ranch on the left.

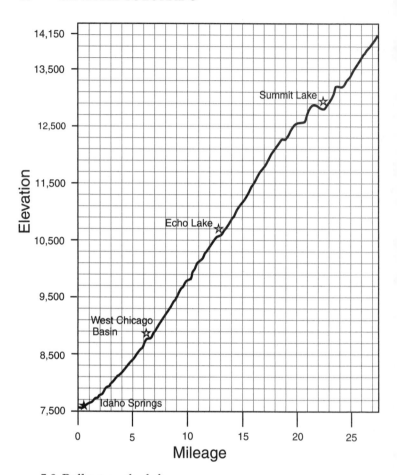

5.0 Pullout on the left.

5.3 Cascade Creek Road.

☆6.4 West Chicago Creek (8,842 feet). The first of many tight turns. Pullout here that makes this a good starting point if you'd like to forego the warm-up along the river. Forest Service campsite and picnic area 2 miles west on the dirt road.

6.8 Large pullout.

7.8 Chicago Forks Picnic Area.

8.5 Christian Prayer Retreat on the right. There is no shoulder, just rutted gravel, should you go off the road.

9.7 Ponder Point Picnic Area.

11.9 Turnout on the right with an overlook.

12.4 Echo Lake Park. The easy(er) part is over. This is a beautiful area.

12.5 Echo Lake.

☆13.0 Junction with Colorado Highway 5 (10,660 feet). Restaurant and souvenir store to the right; campground to the left. Ahead is the road up Mount Evans and a small fee station. Plenty of parking all around. Highway 103 continues east over Juniper and Squaw Passes back down to Fillius Park in Bergen Park (ride 7).

13.3 Sign warning visitors that hunting may be in progress from mid-August to mid-November.

14.0 First big hairpin, 15 mph, gravel on the road.

15.4 Great view of the road ahead. Here (11,400 feet) you begin to climb above timberline. There is little shoulder and the surface is rough.

16.0 Pullout on the left at the trailhead for the Mount Goliath Natural Area.

16.1 Bristlecone pines.

16.3 Good view of the Great Plains, smog, and Squaw Pass, all to the east.

16.4 You are now above tree line for good. Expect wind.

17.9 Pullout to the left at the trailhead for Alpine Gardens Trail No. 49.

18.0 Divots in the road.

18.9 Rough road, but there is a good view ahead.

19.0 A rock wall sheds debris onto the road.

19.1 The road flattens out. It is warmer and less windy on the southern side of the mountain.

20.0 Good view of Pikes Peak and Denver to the east.

20.6 The grade picks up again and there is a lot of rockfall on the road.

21.8 Gradual descent to Summit Lake.

☆22.3 Summit Lake (12,840 feet). Large parking area, small hut, some walkways; no boating. It is typically blustery. The wind is usually out of the north so it can be for and against you as you change direction through all the switchbacks.

22.9 The road gets steeper, rougher, and tougher.

23.4 Mile 10 marks a hole in the road. Expect snow or ice.

24.2 Begin a series of switchbacks and go down a bit.

24.5 Head up again. There's good views out west and it's windy.

24.8 Good view of South Park.

25.3 A hole and gravel pile are in the down-coming lane.

25.4 The first glimpse of the observatory (the top).

25.6 Very steep.

26.0 The final approach to the summit.

28.2 Road end (14,150 feet), shy of the actual summit of Mount Evans. There is even a bike rack.

9   LOVELAND PASS
11,992 feet

Before the Eisenhower Tunnel, Loveland Pass was it. Now Loveland Pass is mostly a scenic bypass, which is good for cyclists because the road offers great hairpins and the feeling of cresting the top of the state. It is also a great place to be on a summer afternoon because the "east side" of the pass actually faces north and is shady and cold. The only drawback to Loveland Pass is that the eastern side is short. There are no bike paths or frontage roads between the Loveland Basin area exit 216 and the Bakerville exit 218 on I-70, so if you want to ride farther on the east side of Loveland, you must deal with two miles on I-70. While it is legal to ride a bike on these two miles, I wouldn't recommend it to anyone because traffic is so thunderous and dangerous.

EAST TO WEST: Distance from Loveland Valley Ski Area to the intersection of U.S. Highway 6 and I-70 in Silverthorne: 20.8 miles

EAST SIDE: Distance from Loveland Valley Ski Area to Loveland Pass: 4.5 miles

Elevation gain: 1,343 feet

Grades: Maximum 9%; average 6.0% for 4.2 miles

Difficulty: 3

WEST SIDE: Distance from Keystone Ski Area to Loveland
    Pass: 8.5 miles

Elevation gain: 2,633 feet

Grades: Maximum 10%; 6% for 8.2 miles

Difficulty: 2

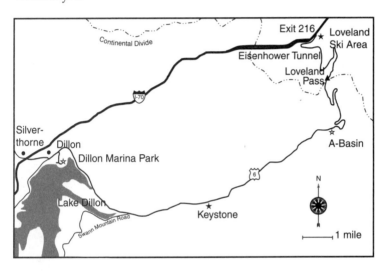

Recommended Start and Stop Points

East Side: Loveland Valley Ski Area parking lot (10,636 feet), exit 216 off I-70; 4.5 miles and 1,343 feet of elevation gain to Loveland Pass. From the exit, turn left down the frontage road to the huge parking areas for skiers. During the summer, there is plenty of space. There is no food or water except for an occasional vending machine near skier facilities. This area is already high, and there is virtually no warm-up for the pass.

West Side: Keystone Ski Area main parking lot (9,359 feet) on U.S. Highway 6, 7.8 miles east of I-70; 8.5 miles and 2,633 feet of elevation gain to Loveland Pass. This is such a large area that there are no facilities just out of the car, but 0.5 mile west, Rasor Lane has drugstores and restaurants.

Looking down the east side of Loveland Pass.

Alternate Start and Stop Points

West Side: Dillon Marina Park and Amphitheater (9,038 feet), on Lake Dillon Drive; 15 miles and 2,954 feet of elevation gain to Loveland Pass. From I-70 take exit 205 and follow U.S.

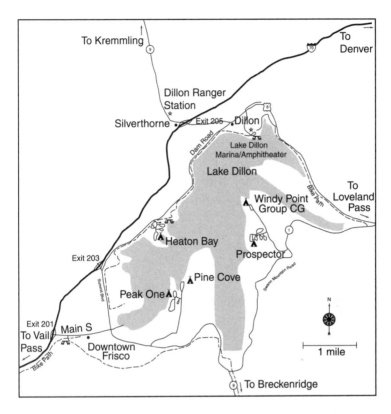

Highway 6 east 1.1 miles to the intersection of Evergreen Road to the left (north) and Lake Dillon Drive. Turn right onto Lake Dillon Drive. In 0.3 mile, reach a T intersection with Lodgepole. Turn left, and immediately to the right is a large parking area for the Marina Park (to the right on Lodgepole is another parking area with no facilities). This is an excellent place to start from the west because it adds nearly 7 miles of good warm-up. The road from here to the Keystone Ski Area is studded with stop lights and traffic, but the road also has a huge shoulder. (You can bypass part of the highway by taking the bike path that parallels it, joining Swann Mountain Road near Swann and U.S. Highway 6.) The Dillon Marina Park is an elaborate place with picnic tables, rest rooms, and water, all well shaded and overlooking Lake Dillon.

Arapaho Basin Ski Area (10,766 feet) on U.S. Highway 6, 12.75 miles east of I-70; 3.6 miles and 1,226 feet of elevation gain to Loveland Pass. The area is hard to miss because it is near a winding curve, and there is usually a row of flags that make good wind indicators. Starting from here makes the west side roughly equivalent to the east side. The place is fairly empty in the summer. Behind the rows of Euro flags are cafes, rest rooms, first aid, and parking.

Road and Traffic Conditions

Traffic on Loveland Pass is slower and more polite than on most roads, and there are few trucks. Despite its altitude and secondary status due to Interstate 70, the road is well maintained. The east side is not a good choice for early or late in the season because it is cold and shady, and windblown snow forms water-covered ice. Even in summer, there is more debris and gravel on the east than the west. In the last 0.5 mile before the summit, the east side has no shoulder and the road is rough. West of the pass, the road has more shoulder, and is in good shape with few cracks and bumps.

Descents

The grades on both sides are uniform, so the road is fast.

West Side: Faster than the east, having longer straightaways and fewer surprises.

East Side: The turns are sharp enough that you'll go through them faster than the cars, and using the whole lane comes easily.

Sleep and Supplies

This is a pretty civilized area. The eastern side is in Clear Creek County; for more information call the Clear Creek County Tourism Board, 800-882-5278 or 303-567-4660. The western side is in Summit County; for more information call 970-668-2051.

The area is in the White River National Forest, Dillon Ranger District, 303-468-5400. There is no camping near the pass or on the eastern side, but there is quite a bit around Lake Dillon (see the Lake Dillon area map). Windy Point and Prospector Campgrounds are on the east shore off Colorado Highway 1/Swann Mountain Road (reachable from the Marina Park via the bike path paralleling U.S. Highway 6). Pine Cove and Peak One Campgrounds are on the south shore off Highway 1/Swann Mountain Road near Frisco. Heaton Bay Campground and Picnic Area are on the west shore off the Dam Road and bike path between Dillon and Frisco.

MILEAGE LOG

★0.0 Loveland Valley Ski Area parking lot (10,636 feet). Acres of space in the summer.

0.2 I-70 exit ramp meets with the short frontage road.

0.5 Sign reading "Loveland Pass summit, 4 miles, Loveland Basin Ski area, Arapaho National Forest."

0.6 Begin the turn, cross under the chairlift, and start going uphill. No stopping or standing in this area.

0.7 Early or late in the season there is sand, gravel, and ice in the shadows.

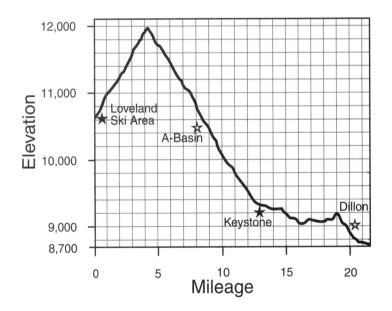

1.2 Already you've climbed about 350 feet, to 11,000 feet.

1.3 Middle of 30 mph curve. Things get sunnier and drier.

2.0 The 20 mph curve is steep and nicely banked.

3.0 Gravel, no shoulder, rough road, big drop-offs.

▲4.5 Loveland Pass (11,992 feet). Big signs, steep grades, good views. A few places to pull over. The west side is brighter and warmer.

5.3 Crest of first steep curve. There is not much danger of rocks and other large debris on this road because it is not cut deeply into the mountainside.

7.75 Last-chance parking area.

☆8.1 Arapaho Basin Ski Area (10,766 feet). Cafes, rest rooms, first aid, parking behind rows of Euro flags. There are many "no parking" signs along the road near the ski area.

10.0 Pullout on the left. Stacked Jersey barriers.

12.2 Shady, sometimes icy.

12.6 Keystone Ski Area comes into view.

★13.0 First turnoff into Keystone's humongous parking area (9,359 feet).

13.5 Rasor Lane. Mountain View Drugs, many facilities and restaurants are everywhere.

14.7 Gas and grocery.

16.3 Intersection with Swann Mountain Road/Colorado Highway 1 (leads to Colorado Highway 9 between Frisco and Breckenridge).

16.6 Cross Snake River.

17.25 Dillon City Limit.

18.9 East entrance to Dillon.

19.5 Upper turnoff to Lake Dillon Marina, Museum, Amphitheater.

☆19.7 Intersection with Evergreen Road to the right, Lake Dillon Drive to the left—turn left to end the ride at the Marina Park (9,038 feet); the main route continues straight on U.S. Highway 6 to Silverthorne.

20.1 Big intersection with Dam Road to the left. City Market, Gart Brothers, and towering signs. To the left, the road goes out over the dam; continue straight on U.S. Highway 6.

20.8 Intersection with I-70; continue straight on U.S. Highway 6.

21.1 Intersection with Wildernest Road to the left and Rainbow Drive to the right. Continue straight ahead; you are now on Colorado Highway 9 headed north.

21.6 Intersection with Sixth Street in Silverthorne. Town Hall on the left; Forest Service Information Center/Dillon Ranger Station on the right—here you can find maps to all the bikeways of the area.

10 VAIL PASS
10,600 feet

Vail Pass is the most civilized and recreational pass in the state. It is the only one with a bike path, which saves you from riding on Interstate 70, and the path changes the entire character of the ride. Vail Pass is a meandering ride in the woods instead of a long push up a big hill. On the east side, the path is below the highway and closely follows West Tenmile Creek. You can always hear the traffic of the interstate, but at times you can't see it, which creates an illusion of wilderness. The west side is more varied. The path sometimes sticks next to the freeway racing straight down, and other times it twists through hemlocks and dark woods. The weather limits Vail Pass much more than other passes; snow lingers well into late spring.

EAST TO WEST: Distance from Wheeler Flats to Bighorn Park: 16.9 miles
EAST SIDE: Distance from Wheeler Flats to Vail Pass: 6.1 miles
Elevation gain: 905 feet
Grades: Maximum 6.0%; average 3.0% for 2.2 miles, 3.5% for 3.2 miles
Difficulty: 1

WEST SIDE: Distance from Gore Creek Campground to Vail
    Pass: 9.7 miles
Elevation gain: 1,872 feet
Grades: Maximum 7%; 5% for 4.3 miles, 6.6% for 2.6 miles
Difficulty: 2

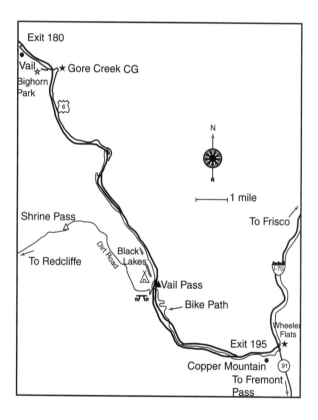

Recommended Start and Stop Points

East Side: Wheeler Flats Trailhead (9,700 feet), on Colorado
Highway 91 south of I-70; 6.1 miles and 905 feet of elevation
gain to Vail Pass. From I-70 take the Copper Mountain exit/exit
195 and head south on Highway 91 to the main entrance to the
Copper Mountain Ski Area. To the left is a small road that leads
past a gas station, and at its end is the Wheeler Flats trailhead

The end of the Vail Pass Bike Trail near Copper Mountain.

parking area. There are no facilities here, but it is uncrowded and well located, and you're never far from a convenience store on I-70. From here, the bike path leads west to Vail Pass (to the east, it heads back to Frisco).

West Side: Gore Creek Campground (8,728 feet) east of I-70 less than 2 miles south of exit 180; 9.7 miles and 1,872 feet of elevation gain to Vail Pass. From I-70 take exit 180 and go east on Bighorn Road as it curves around and goes under the interstate. In less than 2 miles reach Gore Creek Campground; a locked gate is where the road becomes U.S. Highway 6. There is a lot of parking here and a lot of people making use of it. There is no water or rest room availability except inside the campground.

Alternate Start and Stop Points

West Side: Bighorn Park (8,518 feet) west of I-70 less than 2 miles south of exit 180; 10.8 miles and 2,082 feet of elevation gain to Vail Pass. From I-70 take exit 180 and drive south on Bighorn Road about 1 mile, almost to where it crosses under the interstate; turn right at Main Gore Drive. Turn right again at

The west side of the Vail Pass Bike Trail.

Juniper Lane and continue 0.3 mile farther to Meadow Drive and the park. This is a more pleasant, relaxed, and less crowded spot than Gore Creek Campground. There are no bighorns but plenty of grass, a little parking, rest rooms, and a weak water fountain.

Road and Traffic Conditions

You'll be sharing the path with everyone from hikers to in-line skaters, and it is narrow enough to make passing slow. The path is in good shape and free of the usual gravel and road debris you might find on a highway. The first few miles out of Copper Mountain, however, have lots of debris. On the west side, in some places the path is old U.S. Highway 6 and the road is still in good shape, wide and clean. Believe signs warning of closed gates or blind curves. Because the path is tucked away, the first snow stays until the beginning of summer.

Descents

West or east, for all but the last 4 miles of the west side of the path, be ready to stop. At any moment, you may round a corner and find people stopped in the path eating, looking around, or resting. Even if you have the path to yourself, the tight curves are unbanked.

West Side: The last 4 miles are steep, straight, and wide open.

East Side: See the first paragraph above.

Riding up Vail Pass.

Sleep and Supplies

There are plenty of convenience stores near Wheeler Flats, so sodas, water, and snacks are never far away at the beginning of this ride.

The east side is in Summit County, so for more information call 970-668-2051; for the west side, call Vail Valley Tourism and Convention Bureau, 800-525-3875 or 970-476-1000.

The bike path is in the White River National Forest, 970-945-2521, Holy Cross Ranger District, 970-827-5715. There are some campsites near the Black Lakes close to the summit, but the site nearest the bike path is Gore Creek Campground.

MILEAGE LOG

★0   Wheeler Flats Trailhead (9,700 feet) immediately south of Copper Mountain. Head north on the bike path or road and then head west to work your way through Copper Mountain.

0.25 Gas station.

0.3 Another parking area, which is just as good as the one at Wheeler Flats Trailhead.

0.4 Enter the town of Copper Mountain and pass an information kiosk.

0.75 Intersection with Wheeler Road. You are on Copper Road. Head toward the white tennis dome.

1.0 Intersection with Ten Mile Circle Road.

1.5 Continue past the Telemark Lodge to the end of Copper Mountain Road.

1.8 Beginning of the bike trail. A small parking area here is aggressively signed "Stables Parking Only." As you begin

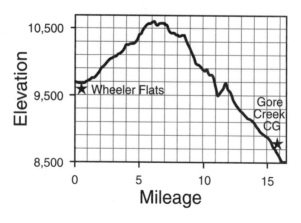

up this trail, expect a lot of gravel, horse manure, and people—but it gets better as you go.

2.3 Speed bump and washout.

4.7 Sharp switchbacks. The pass comes into view.

6.0 Tunnel into the rest-area complex. Expect a lot of water, broken glass, and other trash on the path inside the tunnel.

▲ 6.1 Vail Pass (10,600 feet). An elaborate parking area with rest rooms, water. Zigzag around back to the on-ramp and then head down old U.S. Highway 6. Follow the green sign for the bike route. The Shrine Pass Road (dirt) heads north just before U.S. 6. Old U.S. 6 is a bit bumpy but not bad. The road is a series of steps that level out at the Black Lakes.

7.6 Dam parking area; west of Black lakes. A sign here tells you to slow down, which seems dumb at first, but just around the corner is a gate that is always closed and much sturdier than a bike frame. There are a few campsites here, but they are usually full during the summer.

7.9 The road ends and turn back into a bike path.

10.0 The path parallels I-70 and is very steep.

11.9 Steep section ends and the path passes under the interstate to the north side, where it winds through trees and goes back up toward old U.S. 6. Through this section, you're likely to round a corner and be faced with a group of people stopped in the middle of the path.

12.1 Path rejoins U.S. 6, marked by a large green sign reading "Recreation Trail." The next few miles down are fast and wide open.

15.75 Gate; always closed, and many vehicles will be parked here.

☆ 15.8 Gore Creek Campground (8,728 feet), White River National Forest. Plenty of parking, plus campsites. U.S. 6 becomes Bighorn Road when you reach the town of Vail.

16.3 Intersection with Main Gore Drive. Turn left down Main Gore Drive to reach Bighorn Park.

16.6 Intersection with Juniper Lane. Turn right down Juniper Lane.

★16.9 Intersection with Meadow Drive at Bighorn Park (8,518 feet). No bighorns, but plenty of grass, a little parking, rest rooms, an anemic water fountain. This is less crowded than Gore Creek Campground.

11 KENOSHA and RED HILL PASSES
9,994 and 10,030 feet

Kenosha Pass is distinguished by variety and convenience. The road follows the North Fork of the South Platte River, but there are plenty of steep sections. It is close to Denver, but the top has excellent camping, and from here you can see row upon row of mountains, each lit a different color by the twilight. Red Hill Pass is the smallest pass in the state, going over a hogback, not a mountain range. Still, it is well positioned and gives great views of South Park. It makes a nice add-on to Kenosha Pass when the weather is warm, but in an autumn or spring storm, South Park is no place to be.

EAST TO WEST: Distance from Bailey Town Park to Fairplay Town Park: 39 miles

EAST SIDE: Distance from Bailey Town Park to Kenosha Pass: 18.6 miles

Elevation gain: To Kenosha Pass, 2,212 feet; to Red Hill Pass, 486 feet

Grades: Kenosha Pass, maximum 6.5%, average 2.8% for 3.7 miles, 4.6% for 4 miles; Red Hill Pass, average 5.3% for 1.7 miles

Difficulty: 3

WEST SIDE: Distance from Jefferson to Kenosha Pass: 4.3 miles

Elevation gain: Red Hill Pass, 269 feet; Kenosha Pass, 452 feet

Grades: Red Hill Pass, 4.5% for 1.1 miles; Kenosha Pass, maximum 5.1%, average 5.1% for 1.2 miles

Difficulty: 1

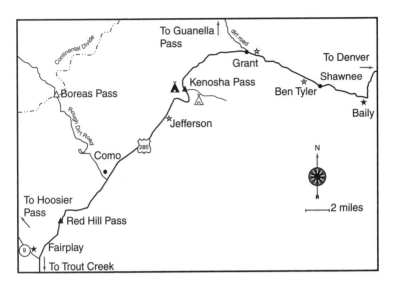

Recommended Start and Stop Points

East Side: Bailey Town Park (7,780 feet) off U.S. Highway 285 behind the feed store; 18.6 miles and 2,212 feet of elevation gain to Kenosha Pass. The Bailey Town Park is a funky little place. There is not much in the way of shade, but there is a boat without water, a caboose without tracks, and a bridge in need of a road. There are many signs forbidding parking after dark and warning against trespassing after business hours. Nearby facilities include a Laundromat, food stores, camping supplies.

West Side: Jefferson (9,500 feet) on U.S. Highway 285; 4.3 miles and 452 feet of elevation gain to Kenosha Pass. Jefferson, the closest town to Kenosha Pass, is too small to have any real public areas, but there is parking near an abandoned gas station on the west side of the highway. Jefferson has snacks, coffee, gifts, and a gas station that is not self-service.

Alternate Start and Stop Points

East Side: Ben Tyler Trailhead (8,455 feet) on the south side of U.S. Highway 285, 2 miles west of the town of Shawnee; 11.7 miles and 1,575 feet of elevation gain to Kenosha Pass.

Cresting Red Hill.

Starting from here eliminates the lower, hotter portion of the ride, and is a good place to start for a 64.2-mile out-and-back to Fairplay.

Pullout (8,649 feet) on U.S. Highway 285, 0.4 mile east of Grant; 7.8 miles and 1,381 feet of elevation gain to Kenosha Pass. Parking in Grant is for residents and customers only, but there is easy parking at the pullout. The Guanella Pass road starts at Grant, but unfortunately it is dirt.

West Side: Town park at Fourth and Main in central Fairplay (9,935 feet)—home to the World Champion Pack Burro Race—north of the junction of U.S. Highway 285 and Colorado Highway 9; 20.4 miles and 59 feet of elevation gain to Kenosha Pass. There is a prominent red-brick library in the town park that has plenty of parking, a few benches, and wide expanses of grass. There are a few picnic tables, but rest rooms and water are inside the library, which may or may not be open.

Road and Traffic Conditions

U.S. Highway 285 is a busy place, especially eastbound on a

Sunday afternoon. At times the traffic is so bad that although you won't be in danger of being hit, you may be overcome by the fumes spewing out of bumper-to-bumper vehicles. Ride Kenosha Pass in the morning or on a weekday. The road is in good shape and has a fair amount of fresh pavement and adequate shoulders. Near the top, however, the shoulders have been cut up with vibration stripes that keep sleepy motorists on the road. People like to travel fast when they can on this road.

Descents

West Side: You'll be down Kenosha Pass before you have time to adjust your helmet and change gears.

East Side: Kenosha Pass is a lot of fun because of the varying grade. Push through the flatter sections, and you can count on intermittent steepness to keep up a good constant speed. The turns up top are good too.

Sleep and Supplies

Small stores, bars, and restaurants are always nearby on U.S. Highway 285, in the towns of Bailey (Laundromat, food stores, camping supplies, and a place to hire attorneys or guns,

Heading east over Kenosha Pass.

depending on how things are going), Shawnee (store and trading post), Grant (restaurant and lounge), Jefferson (snacks, coffee, gifts, and a gas station that is not self-service), Como (mercantile, general store, and a bed and breakfast), and Fairplay (liquor and sporting goods stores, a few eateries and hotels, a convenience store complex). Lodging is a bit rarer but it's there. This entire ride is within Park County. For more information call the South Park Chamber of Commerce, 303-836-4279, or if you're farther east, the Conifer Chamber of Commerce, 303-838-0178.

The area is in Pike National Forest, 719-545-8737, within the South Platte Ranger District, 303-275-5610. The lower part of Kenosha Pass is all private land, so no luck camping until the top of Kenosha Pass. There is a good campground west of the road, and a picnic area east of the road has picnic tables, water, and access to the Colorado Trail, as well as excellent dispersed camping a bit to its east, so there is something for everybody. This is a fairly popular area, but there is still always plenty of room somewhere in the aspens. The Michigan Creek Forest Service road leads west from Jefferson to camping after only 2 miles of extremely rough dirt road.

MILEAGE LOG

★0   Bailey Town Park (7,782 feet). Head out of town on U.S. Highway 285.

0.3 Bailey's west end. Gas station, restaurant, pizza.

1.2 Fishing hole on the left.

2.15 Pullout on the right and another fishing hole, this one shaded.

2.7 Mooredale Road.

4.9 The town of Shawnee. Store and Trading Post, but no public areas.

☆6.9 Ben Tyler Trailhead (8,455 feet). Nothing here but parking. This is a good alternate start if you want to eliminate the flatter parts of the ride to the east or shorten the ride all the way to Red Hill Pass or Fairplay.

9.4 Camp Santa Maria, a Catholic Community Services camp.

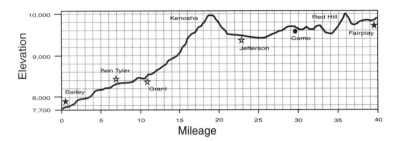

☆10.8 Best pullout near Grant and a good alternate start (8,649 feet).

11.2 The town of Grant and intersection with the Guanella Pass Road. Restaurant and lounge but not much else. There is little parking along the highway, and that is posted as only for residents and customers.

11.7 Pullout on the right.

11.9 Cross Robert's Tunnel outlet. Good shoulder, which is a good thing here.

14.0 Good shoulder but beware vibration strips.

15.4 Fresh pavement begins.

16.0 Intermittent shoulder, smooth road, nice turns, bad gravel in spring. A stream is nearby.

17.3 Forest Service Road 810 on the right.

17.9 Respectably steep.

▲18.6 Kenosha Pass (9,994 feet), a big area that sports several campgrounds. To the east is a huge day-use area with picnic tables, water, and access to the Colorado Trail, where you can park for $4 (or park along the highway for free). Dispersed camping is allowed just beyond the day-use area, or there is a larger pay camping area on the west side of the road. This is a fairly popular area, but there is still always plenty of room somewhere in the aspens. Traffic at the top is extremely fast. Jarring vibration strips are cut into the pavement near the summit on both sides of the pass.

18.9 Pullout on the left near a sign for Pike National Forest. Only a slight grade.

19.0 Pullout.

19.3 Pullouts on both sides of the road.

19.9 Steep, couple of good turns. That's about it for the west side of Kenosha Pass.

20.1 Good pullout, excellent view.

21.7 Forest Service Lost Park Road on the left.

★22.9 The town of Jefferson (9,500 feet). Gas and sodas here.

24.8 Park County Road 35, mile 197.

28.6 Good pavement and good views all around.

29.0 Elk Meadows road.

29.4 Road to Como and Boreas Pass on the right. Como is well situated about 0.5 mile down the road; mercantile, general store, and a bed and breakfast.

31.5 Pullout.

32.7 Park County Road 7.

▲35.1 Top of Red Hill Pass (10,030 feet).

38.5 Intersection with Colorado Highway 9 just outside Fairplay; a convenience-store complex here. Good views of Colorado's big, broad mountains. The road surface is poor, but the shoulder is adequate.

☆39.0 Turn right on Highway 9 to reach Park County Library and Town Park at the corner of Fourth and Hathaway in central Fairplay (9,935 feet). Plenty of parking, a few benches, and wide expanses of grass, but the only rest rooms or water is in the library, which may or may not be open.

12 HOOSIER PASS
11,541 feet

Hoosier Pass is proof that moderate is not mediocre. It's a great ride on either side and gets so close to mountaintops that it feels more like a curving detour to tree line than an efficient way through the mountains. The north side has the sharpest curves in the area, and although some passes are great for pushing speed, the north side of Hoosier is a great test of cornering ability. It's everything a good pass should be, and convenient to boot.

NORTH TO SOUTH: Distance from Breckenridge to Fairplay Town Park: 27.1 miles

NORTH SIDE: Distance from Breckenridge to Hoosier Pass: 9.5 miles

Elevation gain: 1,894 feet

Grades: Maximum 7.9%; average 2.2% for 5.5 miles, 5.9% for 4 miles

Difficulty: 3

SOUTH SIDE: Distance from Fairplay Town Park to Hoosier Pass: 11 miles

Elevation gain: 1,574 feet

Grades: Maximum 7.8%; 5.5% for 3.7 miles

Difficulty: 2

Recommended Start and Stop Points

North Side: Intersection of Colorado Highway 9 and Broken Lance Road near the southern edge of Breckenridge (9,647 feet); 9.5 miles and 1,894 feet to Hoosier Pass. There is ample public parking 0.5 mile north of here and scattered throughout town.

South Side: Town park at Fourth and Main in central Fairplay (9,935 feet)—home to the World Champion Pack Burro Race—north of the junction of Colorado Highway 9 with U.S. Highway 285; 11 miles and 1,574 feet to Hoosier Pass. There is a

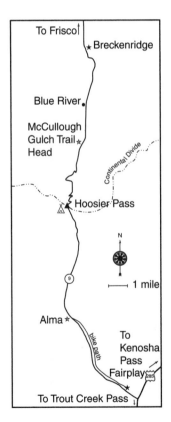

prominent red-brick library in the town park, which has plenty of parking, a few benches, and wide expanses of grass. There are a few picnic tables, but rest rooms and water are inside the library, which may or may not be open.

Alternate Start and Stop Points

North Side: McCullough Gulch Trailhead (10,287 feet) on the west side of Colorado Highway 9; 3.9 miles and 1,254 feet of elevation gain to Hoosier Pass. The site is easily found because it is across the highway from a ski lodge/bar. There are two roads: one immediately north, which is private, and the proper road, which is marked by a sign. This is the trailhead for Quandary Peak. There is plenty of parking, but no facilities. It's a pity that camping is not allowed because it sure would be a good spot.

South Side: Alma (10,578 feet), on the west side of Colorado Highway 9; 5.3 miles and 1,204 feet of elevation gain to Hoosier Pass. There isn't a single public parking area in Alma, but there are a few places on side streets and along the highway. Alma, a small town that seems impervious to the

Good curves and grades on the north side of Hoosier Pass.

ski/art gallery industries that fill the storefronts in so many mountain towns, is a contrast with Breckenridge, but anything needed can be found here.

Road and Traffic Conditions

The north side is a bit congested because it is fairly narrow, heavily curved, and well traveled by both long-distance and local traffic. There are many driveways and side streets, and dirt and gravel spill onto the highway. The shoulder is minimal where it is needed most, but it shows up in the straightaways. The south side is much straighter and simpler. A bike path that runs between Alma and Fairplay is not that bad.

Descents

South Side: A fast, fairly straight coast into South Park on a road that is ample and in good shape. There are a couple steep sections, but these don't last long. Once you reach Alma, it's pretty flat and there is a bike path between Alma and Fairplay.

North Side: More interesting because the road is steep and wildly curved. The switchbacks are stacked on top of each other, and you can easily see the next curve from above.

Sleep and Supplies

Food and services are available in Breckenridge, Alma, and Fairplay (liquor and sporting goods stores, a few eateries and hotels); don't look for anything in the little town of Blue River. There is lots of lodging but little camping. The northern side is in Summit County, so for more information call the Summit County Chamber of Commerce, 970-668-2051. The southern side is in Park County, and Fairplay is most of what's there. For more information call the South Park Chamber of Commerce, 303-836-4279.

North of the pass is in White River National Forest, 303-468-5400. South of the pass is in Pike National Forest, 719-836-2031. Other than good dispersed camping just to the west of the summit, there's no camping along this route; you'll have to keep going somewhere else to pitch a tent.

MILEAGE LOG

★0   Colorado Highway 9 at Broken Lance Road near the south end of Breckenridge (9,647 feet).

1.4 Town of Blue River. Keep going.

4.4 There's not much shoulder on the big rolling hills and mellow grade alongside the Blue River.

5.1 Sign for Quandary Peak. Start going up.

☆5.6 McCullough Gulch Trailhead road (10,287 feet) on the right. Plenty of parking, no facilities. Camping not allowed.

6.5 Series of 10 mph curves. Expect dirt and gravel near the shoulder.

▲9.5 Hoosier Pass (11,541 feet). Hoosier is what you expect of a Colorado pass: a small spot with long views and a few hulking fourteeners (Lincoln and Bross) looming over your shoulder. There are a few signs telling the history of the place.

13.0 Bottom of grade.

13.15 Intersection of County Road 4 angling back to the right.

☆14.8 Alma city limit (10,578 feet). If you'd rather, take the bike path on the east side of the highway the rest of the way to Fairplay.

16.5 Mosquito Gulch Road to the west.

26.85 Fairplay city limit (9,935 feet).

★27.1 Park County Library and Town Park at the corner of Fourth and Hathaway. Plenty of parking, a few benches, and wide expanses of grass, but the only rest rooms or water is in

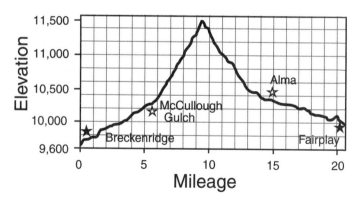

the library, which may or may not be open. (It's another 0.5 mile to the intersection with U.S. Highway 285, with typical gas station and convenience-store fare).

13 FREMONT PASS
11,318 feet

Fremont Pass's broad summit is the site of the Climax molybdenum mine, making it the best Tour de Tailing Ponds in the state. The road is surprisingly straight on both sides of the pass with only a few turns near the summit. The ride is moderate, and the steep sections are not too sustained on the southern side. The northern side is cooler and green with beautiful views just as you begin to gain speed. This side is perfect for biking because it has a huge shoulder; it is a good climb and a fantastic descent.

NORTH TO SOUTH: Distance from Wheeler Flats Trailhead to
    Leadville: 23.9 miles
NORTH SIDE: Distance from Wheeler Flats Trailhead to
    Fremont Pass: 11.4 miles
Elevation gain: 1,618 feet
Grades: Maximum 7.5%; 2.5% for 5.4 miles, 4.5% for 1.7 miles,
    7% for 1.1 miles
Difficulty: 2
SOUTH SIDE: Distance from Leadville to Fremont Pass: 12.5
    miles
Elevation gain: 1,166 feet
Grades: Maximum 7.5%; average 1.4% for 5.8 miles, 4.5% for
    3.7 miles
Difficulty: 2

Recommended Start and Stop Points:
North Side: Wheeler Flats Trailhead (9,700 feet) on Colorado Highway 91 south of Interstate 70; 11.4 miles and 1,618 feet of

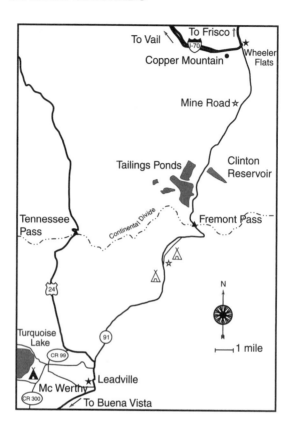

elevation gain to Fremont Pass. Take the Copper Mountain exit/exit 195 off I-70 and head south on Highway 91 to the main entrance to the Copper Mountain Ski Area. To the left is a small road that leads past a gas station, and at its end is the Wheeler Flats Trailhead parking area. There are no facilities here, but it is uncrowded and well located. From here, there's a bike path that leads east to Frisco or west to Vail Pass (ride 10).

South Side: Intersection with Ninth, where U.S. Highway 24 becomes Harrison in Leadville (10,152 feet). The center of town is along Harrison Street. Just west of Ninth and Harrison is the National Mining Museum. There is enough parking in front of the museum, and you can stage here for either Fremont or Tennessee Pass (ride 14).

Alternate Start and Stop Points

North Side: Start of the grade on Colorado Highway 91, 4.2 miles south of Interstate 70, at a large mine road to the right/west (10,231 feet); 7.2 miles and 1,087 feet of elevation gain to Fremont Pass. At the top of the valley, it's easy to see where the grade starts. There is room to park at the intersection of the mining road, or 0.75 mile south there is an ample pullout with better shade. Starting from here cuts out the valley cruise and puts you on the steeps immediately.

South Side: Side road on the east side of Colorado Highway 91 (10,439 feet), 8.9 miles north of Leadville; 3.6 miles and 879 feet of elevation gain to Fremont Pass. This stretch of old paved roadway runs between the highway and Ten Mile Creek for about 2 miles; it can be used as a parking area. There are also small roads within several miles of here leading into the forest that can be used as parking areas or for dispersed camping. This option leaves little distance to the summit, but takes off only about a quarter of the climbing.

Road and Traffic Conditions

If every road were as good as Colorado Highway 91, there would be no conflicts between bikes and cars. The road is straight enough to allow cars to pass each other without the usual foul feelings. The shoulders, especially huge on the north side, allow plenty of room for everyone. On some roads the shoulder is little more than a flat gutter full of sand and broken bottles, but the shoulder on Fremont Pass is as good as a whole lane. It is wide, smooth, clean, and perfect.

Descents

South Side: There is a sharp drop right off the summit, but after that you'll have to work for speed. The road eases into the valley and carries you all the way into Leadville.

North Side: This is the place to tuck. This road is smooth, straight, and steep. The only thing to slow you down is loose clothing and the urge to look at distant peaks instead of the on-rushing road.

Sleep and Supplies

In terms of food and lodging, Fremont is well anchored on both sides but there's not much in the middle. At Wheeler Flats on the north side, there are no facilities, but you're not far from a convenience store on Interstate 70. On the south end, Leadville has much to offer cyclists: camping, coffee, lodging, liquor, history, and rib-sticking breakfasts—all at an elevation higher than many passes. There is a bike store at Ninth and Harrison in Leadville. The north side is within Summit County, 970-668-2051; for more information in the Leadville area, call 719-486-3900.

The area to the west of the pass is part of the San Isabel National Forest, 719-545-8737, and the Leadville Ranger District, 719-486-0749. There is some dispersed camping along the highway, but the only established campsites (about a half dozen) are in the Turquoise Lake area west of Leadville. There are several ways to reach the Turquoise Lake area. From the north, Lake County Road 99 intersects U.S. Highway 24, 1.7 miles north of Highway 24's intersection with Colorado Highway 91. Turn west, and CR 99 leads past condos and lodges before reaching Turquoise Lake. From downtown Leadville, take Sixth Street west to a T intersection with McWethy. Turn right and continue west. South of town, County Road 300 hits U.S. Highway 24 about 4 miles south of Ninth and Harrison in Leadville. Go west 0.4 mile and then turn right.

MILEAGE LOG

★0   Wheeler Flats Trailhead (9,700 feet) immediately south of Copper Mountain.

0.5 Intersection with Copper Mountain Road. All the parking you could dream of.

1.25 Copper Mountain comes into view.

2.5 Road rolls along Ten Mile Creek. There is no shoulder here and the road is fairly rough.

3.5 Large pullout on the left.

☆4.2 Mine road on the right (10,231 feet); steep section begins. The road is still climbing but the grade increases significantly. This is a good alternate start if you want to shave miles and get right to the climbing.

4.6 The road is straight and steep (descending the north side, this is a good place to try for an all-time maximum speed).

7.9 Bridge. The road here is fantastic. There are huge shoulders on either side, guardrails, and a great surface.

8.1 Grade steepens.

9.1 Going up for good.

9.4 Cross gorge, tailings ponds.

▲ 11.4 Fremont Pass (11,318 feet). The Climax Mine, putting the "moly" in chrome-molybdenum bike frames. The pass is broad and flat. There is information on the mine and a few toilets.

12.2 40 mph curve.

☆ 13.2 An old paved road runs along the left (east) side of the highway. There is good informal camping along this road and it can be used as an alternate start.

14.5 Forest Service road on the right.

15.0 Lower road on the left rejoins the highway.

16.3 Colorado Belle Ranch.

16.5 A few curves and the grade picks up.

20.0 The Prospector, a complete supper club. The pavement is good and the shoulder here is great, a full 3 feet wide.

21.0 Marshland and willows. Valley bottom.

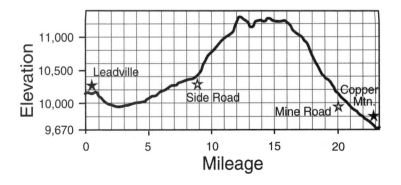

22.4 Sign reads "Climax 12, Frisco 30, Denver 111." Climb a bit.

22.8 Intersection with U.S. Highway 24 (the road to Tennessee Pass).

23.1 National Forest Information Center.

23.9 Intersection of Ninth and Harrison in Leadville. Twenty-fourth becomes Poplar Street in Leadville. From the north, signs lead to the Healy House Museum.

14 TENNESSEE PASS
10,424 feet

Tennessee Pass is unusual because most of the elevation is gained far away from the pass. The steepest portion of the north side is going up the Battle Mountain summit, and although there is still plenty of elevation to gain, there is plenty of mileage too. There's not much to the south side, but descending into Leadville just after sunrise should not be missed—the central Sawatch Mountains look good in the first morning light.

Making good time on Tennessee Pass.

U.S. Highway 24 is also the Tenth Mountain Division memorial highway. The remnants of Camp Hale, its main training ground, are plain to see, and there are many plaques and markers describing the men and missions of the Tenth.

NORTH TO SOUTH: Distance from Holy Cross Ranger Station to downtown Leadville: 32.2 miles

NORTH SIDE: Distance from Holy Cross Ranger Station to Tennessee Pass: 22.4 miles

Elevation gain: 2,684 feet

Grades: Maximum 7.5%; average 1.5% for 5 miles, 4% for 2.1 miles, 4.3% for 5 miles, 6% for 4.8 miles

Difficulty: 3

SOUTH SIDE:

Distance from downtown Leadville to Tennessee Pass: 9.8 miles

Elevation gain: 272 feet

Grades: Maximum 4%; 2.7% for 2.7 miles

Difficulty: 1

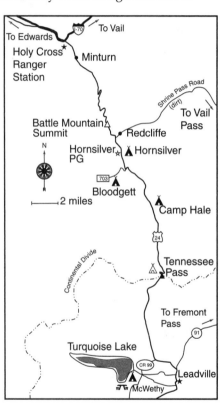

Recommended Start and Stop Points

North Side: Holy Cross Ranger Station (7,740 feet), at exit 171 off Interstate 70; 22.4 miles and 2,684 feet of elevation gain to Tennessee Pass). Look for signs to Minturn to pick up U.S. Highway 24. The White River National Forest ranger station is

It's all downhill from here.

on the right (west) side of the road, with a huge parking area around it. It can't be missed and can't be filled. The station has the usual allotment of maps, camping info, rest rooms, and a water fountain.

South Side: Intersection with Ninth, where U.S. Highway 24 becomes Harrison, in Leadville (10,152 feet); 8.8 miles and 272 feet of elevation gain to Tennessee Pass. The center of town is along Harrison Street. Just west of Ninth and Harrison is the National Mining Museum; there is enough parking in front of the museum. It is a good place to start up either Tennessee or Fremont Pass (ride 13).

Alternate Start and Stop Points
North Side: Hornsilver Campground and Picnic Area (8,748 feet) on the east side of U.S. Highway 24, 11.4 miles south of the Holy Cross Ranger Station in Minturn; 11 miles and 1,676 feet of elevation gain to Tennessee Pass. This large Forest Service campsite has a picnic area right across the road for day use. This is a great alternate start because it cuts the ride in half and cuts out the ups and downs of Battle Mountain.

Road and Traffic Conditions

Traffic on U.S. Highway 24 can be heavy in the morning and evening when workers are commuting between Leadville and the Vail valley. At other times, traffic is surprisingly light for such a major road. U.S. 24 is an old road that has been well maintained. It is narrow, but the surface is good for its entire length. There is enough shoulder for a bike, and the road is not curved enough to make vehicles' passing a problem.

Descents

South Side: Descending is sleepy. Mount Massive dominates the skyline, which is at its best at dawn.

North Side: A series of descents, and whenever it is steep, it is curved. Fortunately, the climb back up Battle Mountain is not so bad and well worth it. The final shot down is nonstop careening.

Sleep and Supplies

Food, beverages, and other supplies can be found in Minturn (plenty of restaurants and a few picnic areas) to the north and Leadville (coffee, liquor, history, and rib-sticking breakfasts all at an elevation higher than many passes) to the south. Leadville has much to offer cyclists, including a bike store at Ninth and Harrison. For more information, call the Greater Leadville Area Chamber of Commerce, 719-456-3900.

The north side of the ride is in the White River National Forest, 970-945-2521. The recommended start for the ride is also the headquarters for the Holy Cross Ranger District, 970-827-5715. The south side is in the San Isabel Forest and part of the Leadville Ranger District, 719-486-0749. On the north side, Hornsilver and Camp Hale Campgrounds are both on the east side of the highway; near Hornsilver is Blodgett Campground, 0.5 mile off the highway. There is dispersed camping on the west side of the pass. There are no campsites on the south side except Turquoise Lake west of Leadville. There are several ways to reach the Turquoise Lake area. From the north, Lake County Road 99 intersects U.S. Highway 24, 1.7 miles north

Heading into Leadville.

of Highway 24's intersection with Colorado Highway 91. Turn west and CR 99 leads past condos and lodges before reaching Turquoise Lake. From downtown Leadville, take Sixth Street west to a T intersection with McWethy. Turn right and continue west. South of town, County Road 300 hits U.S. Highway 24 about 4 miles south of Ninth and Harrison in Leadville. Go west 0.4 mile and then turn right.

MILEAGE LOG

★0   Holy Cross Ranger Station (7,740 feet) on the right side of U.S. Highway 24, off I-70 exit 171. Parking, maps, rest rooms, water fountain.

1.5 Sign says "Welcome to Minturn." Restaurants; a few picnic areas.

2.2 Picnic spot.

4.7 Tigawan Road; Forest Service access.

4.9 Curves and an intermittent shoulder. Expect rocks on the road for the next 5 miles.

5.4 Road gets wider, and the view gets better.

5.9 Large pullout on the right.

6.8 25 mph curves. The road is good for another 2 miles.

△8.3 Battle Mountain Summit (9,235 feet).

9.7 The guardrail and rock wall squeeze the road. Little room for passing.

10.5 Bus stop. Turnoff for the small town of Redcliffe; a small picnic area on the left. Good alternate start/stop point.

☆11.4 Hornsilver NFS Campground (8,748 feet). Good camping or an alternate start/stop point. Picnic area is across the highway.

12.0 Begin to climb again.

12.4 Forest Road 703 and a pay telephone. Blodgett Campground is 0.5 mile down the dirt road. Sharp, 25 mph curves.

7.5 Road 702.

16.9 The remains of Camp Hale, birthplace of the Colorado ski industry.

19.8 Gap in rocks.

21.0 Gas station and cluster of small buildings.

21.7 Series of good curves.

▲22.4 Tennessee Pass (10,424 feet). A good parking area, a road that leads to Ski Cooper ski area, a monument to the Tenth Mountain Division, a few rest rooms.

23.6 Old building on the left. Good spot for pictures.

24.0 Road on the right.

24.7 Sylvan Lakes private community at Lake County Road

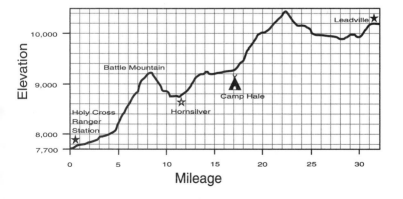

20. Good views, especially in morning light.

25.5 The road flattens as you come into a big, grassy valley at the base of the Collegiate Range.

27.2 Rancho Escondido.

29.3 County Road 99 leads west to the Turquoise Lake area.

31.0 Junction with Colorado Highway 91, which goes north to Fremont Pass (ride 13). Continue on U.S. Highway 24 to Leadville.

31.4 San Isabel National Forest Service Information Center, 2015 N. Poplar. All types of road merchants, gas stations, drive-through liquor stores, small hotels.

★ 32.2 Ninth and Harrison in downtown Leadville (10,152 feet).

15 INDEPENDENCE PASS
12,095 feet

Independence Pass is the fourth-highest chunk of pavement in the state. It has a broad, scenic summit strewn with wildflowers and spotted with pools and sun-warmed stones. Although they share this summit and have similar scenery, the eastern and western sides have very different characters. The eastern half has a short, steep stretch right at the top, but most of the road is a valley cruise. To the west, whether you're going up or down, you'll never have your hands off the handlebars for long. The grade is tough, and the narrow road and convulsive curves thwart any sense of ease.

EAST TO WEST: Distance from Twin Lakes to Maroon Creek
    Road in Aspen: 38.1 miles
EAST SIDE: Distance from Twin Lakes to Independence Pass:
    17.1 miles
Elevation gain: 2,883 feet
Grades: Maximum 6.1%; average 2.8% for 10.7 miles, 5.4% for
    4.4 miles
Difficulty: 4

WEST SIDE: Distance from Difficult Campground to
    Independence Pass: 15.7 miles
Elevation gain: 3,993 feet
Grades: Maximum 6.8%; 3.6% for 6 miles, 5.4% for 6.8 miles,
    6.0% for 2.9 miles
Difficulty: 5

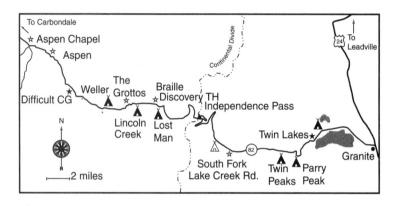

Recommended Start and Stop Points

East Side: The small town of Twin Lakes (9,212 feet) on
Colorado Highway 82, 6 miles west of U.S. Highway 24;
17.1 miles and 2,883 feet of elevation gain to Independence Pass.
The ample parking area for the Twin Lakes National Historic
District is on the south side of the highway in the middle of
town, where there is a large sign. There are picnic tables, rest
rooms, water, and a historic park. Across the street is a gas
station that sells a good assortment of fruit, energy bars, sodas,
candy, and gifts. Highway 82 runs straight through town.

West Side: Difficult Campground (8,100 feet), a few miles
east of Aspen on Highway 82. At a large Forest Service sign
near mile 46, drive east on a paved road for 0.6 mile. Here turn
(straight ahead leads into the camping area) right to park in
a large hikers parking area. It is a beautiful meadow with a
few tables and rest rooms nearby. This is by far the most
pleasant, spacious, and hassle-free starting spot in the Roaring
Fork Valley.

Alternate Start and Stop Points

East Side: South Fork Lake Creek Road (10,130 feet) on Colorado Highway 82, 8.1 miles west of Twin Lakes; 9 miles and 1,965 feet of elevation gain to Independence Pass. This option cuts the mileage in half but saves the best climbing. There are no facilities here, only a parking spot.

West Side: Aspen Chapel (8,100 feet), on the west side of Aspen at the junction of Colorado Highway 82 and the Maroon Creek Road; 21 miles and 4,000 feet of elevation gain to Independence Pass. On any day except

Start of the steep grades on the east side of Independence Pass.

Sunday, there is plentiful, free parking here. At least the sign says, "All are welcome." This start includes a pleasant cruise through town.

Rio Grande Parking Garage (8,100 feet) off Mill and Main Streets in Aspen; 19.7 miles and 4,000 feet of elevation gain to Independence Pass. Follow the blue signs to public parking. A supermarket and shopping center are west of the garage.

The Grottos (9,750 feet) on Colorado Highway 82 near mile 51; 10.4 miles and 2,345 feet of elevation gain to Independence Pass. There is easy but crowded parking along the road near a cliff and steep switchbacks; no other facilities are here. Get here early on weekends.

Braille and Discovery Trailhead (10,282 feet) on Colorado Highway 82, 2 miles east of The Grottos; 7.3 miles and 1,813 feet of elevation gain to Independence Pass. This day-use area has limited parking.

Road and Traffic Conditions

Colorado Highway 82 is generally narrow and rarely has a shoulder, but the pavement is good and smooth. The road cuts deeply into the mountainside for 4 miles on either side of the summit, and grungy rock walls shed debris onto the road. The western side has a notoriously narrow stretch that is 2.3 miles long, running from miles 27 to 29.3. It is difficult to pass on the western side, so drivers are frustrated and aggressive. Vehicles more than 35 feet long are prohibited. Recreational traffic makes for a lot of slow-moving vehicles at campgrounds and trailheads. Weekend traffic is heavy during the summer. Independence Pass is closed in winter, which usually means early November through mid-June, but exact dates are up to Mother Nature. The Leadville Ranger District (see Sleep and Supplies, below) will know if the road is open. The road is sometimes ridable when closed.

Descents

Three miles on either side of the summit have fast straights and brake-burning curves.

West Side: Exciting all the way down. Miles 20 to 26 are not too steep, the grade averaging 3.6 percent, but the lower portion of the canyon more than makes up for this with steep grades and quick hairpins that spice up a constantly weaving road. Do your sightseeing on the way up; you won't have time on the way down. The narrow section from miles 27 to 29.3 is treacherous because there is no extra room if a bike or car is over the center line.

East Side: Mellow after the initial steep 3-mile section.

Sleep and Supplies

Twin Lakes is on the shore of Twin Lakes Reservoir surrounded by the Twin Lakes Recreation Area, with boating, fishing, camping, and various facilities around the reservoir. Twin Lakes has a ready

Independence Pass—almost there!

supply of water, sodas, and snacks. Lodging in Twin Lakes is limited to a few bed and breakfasts. For more information on Twin Lakes, call the Leadville Chamber of Commerce, 719-486-3900.

Aspen has plenty of food as well: There are two convenient supermarkets, one across the street from the Rio Grande Parking Garage at Mill and Main Streets, and City Market at mile 35.5, about 2 miles from the turnoff to Difficult Campground. Everything on the western side is more expensive, more regulated, and less convenient; parking is a fine example. At first glance, Aspen has more parking restriction signs than trees. If you'd like to park in Aspen, go to the Rio Grande Parking Garage off Mill and Main Streets in central Aspen. The attendant can outline official policies. The parking garage opens at 7:00 A.M. and charges 75 cents per hour, but the 7-foot clearance is too low for bikes on roof racks. You can buy a one-day pass for $3 to park in a residential area. A good deal is a carpool pass: If you have three or more people in your car, you can get a carpool pass and park free; from September through Thanksgiving, two people per car earns a carpool pass. Metered rates are $1 per hour. Parking is free everywhere on Sundays and holidays. Fines are high. Aspen's bike stores are mountain bike–oriented. The best place for road gear is Ajax Bike & Sport at Spring and Hyman. For more information on Aspen, call 888-290-1324.

The eastern half of this ride is in the San Isabel National Forest, and there are few, if any restrictions. Call the San Isabel National Forest, Leadville Ranger District, 719-486-0749, for information. The western half is in the White River National Forest, and is dominated by Aspen and its tourism. Call the Aspen Ranger Station, White River National Forest, 970-920-3246. Campgrounds on the east side are clustered around Twin Lakes Reservoir: Twin Lakes, Parry Peak, and Twin Peaks Campgrounds. Camping in the Roaring Fork Canyon on the west side is allowed only in designated sites: Lost Man, Lincoln Creek, Weller, and Difficult Campgrounds. The Forest Service closes the higher-elevation campgrounds as autumn progresses. By October, only Difficult is likely to be open. Call the Aspen Ranger Station about availability. Sites cost $10–12 per night.

Coming down Independence Pass provides lots of speed and little shoulder.

MILEAGE LOG

★0   Twin Lakes National Historic District (9,212 feet) on Colorado Highway 82. At a large sign in the center of town there's an ample parking area with picnic tables, water, rest rooms, and historic buildings. Just across the street is a small gas station that also sells fruit, candy, soda, and gifts. Highway 82 runs straight through town.

2.1 Willis Gulch Trailhead.

4.3 Mount Elbert Lodge, a small bed and breakfast.

6.1 Echo Canyon Road.

☆8.1 South Fork Lake Creek Road (10,130 feet) and parking for the La Plata Trail on the south side of the road. No facilities.

9.1 A good unofficial camping spot on the south side of the road.

12.7 An abrupt, 10 mph curve takes you out of the valley. The real climbing begins here. To the right of this curve is a parking area that leads down to the North Fork Creek.

13.5 From here on up, the road is narrow with no shoulder and a big drop-off. Expect some rocks, gravel, and slight road damage.

17.0 Rude bump in the road.

▲ 17.1 Independence Pass (12,095 feet). Large pullout and parking area. Several trails cross the road. Expect plenty of people.

17.2 Rude bump.

17.7 Rockfall and road damage. The road here is cut deeply into the mountainside. If there aren't rocks on the road, there are liable to be construction crews working to hold them back.

18.6 End of rockfall area.

20.0 Grade eases.

21.2 Prospector townsite. Old mining buildings and pullouts.

23.0 Lost Man Trailhead and campground, White River National Forest.

☆ 24.4 Braille & Discovery Trailhead (10,282 feet). Day use only. Limited parking.

26.5 Lincoln Creek Road 106 on the left (south) side of the road leads to the Lincoln Creek Campground.

27.0 Narrow road, no passing. For 2.3 miles, the road is extremely narrow. There are rock walls on one side and guardrails on the other. There's barely enough room for

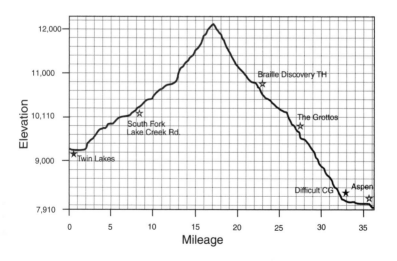

oncoming traffic to pass and precious little room to maneuver.
☆27.5 The Grottos (9,750 feet). Sharp, blind curves and a
pullout with parking.

28.6 Weller Campground.

29.3 End of narrow section.

★32.8 Turnoff for Difficult Campground (8,100 feet) on the
left (south) side of the road, marked by a large Forest Service
sign. From here to mile 34.1, it is illegal to park within 10 feet
of the roadway.

33.2 Grade drops to nil.

34.1 End of no parking area.

34.3 Parking area for the Northstar Nature Preserve. No
overnight parking. Good alternate starting point.

34.7 Small parking area on the right (north) side of the road,
marked off by boulders. No facilities.

35.5 Aspen City Limit.

36.4 Intersection with a City Market on the northwest
corner. Turn right to stay on the highway. There is a sign for
the Rio Grande Parking Garage.

★36.8 Intersection of Mill and Main Streets (8,100 feet). Turn
south at another sign to reach the Rio Grande Parking Plaza.

37.5 White River National Forest Station.

★38.1 Maroon Creek Road turnoff (8,100 feet) to the left. The
Aspen Chapel is visible from here.

16 McCLURE PASS
8,780 feet

The McClure Pass area is gorgeous. The pass,
however, is something of an afterthought. The real attraction
is riding along the Crystal River. This beautiful canyon is cut
into red rock, thick with pine, and always within view of
spectacular white peaks that appear and disappear behind
the nearby hills as you ride over the shadowed road. The pass
is an abrupt division between the central mountains and

mesa and canyon country to the southwest, not to mention differences between the resort towns to the north and the mining towns to the south.

NORTH TO SOUTH: Distance from Carbondale to Paonia: 62.4 miles

NORTH SIDE: Distance from Carbondale to McClure Pass: 25.4 miles

Elevation gain: 2,610 feet

Grades: Maximum 8.7%; average 1.1% for 21.7 miles, 6.8% for 3.4 miles

Difficulty: 2

SOUTH SIDE: Distance from Paonia State Park to McClure Pass: 13.4 miles

Elevation gain: 2,045 feet

Grades: Maximum 7.3%; 1% for 8.3 miles, 5.7% for 5.1 miles

Difficulty: 1

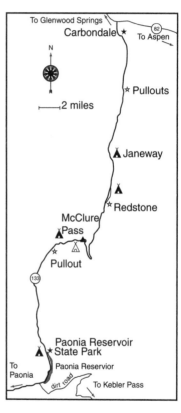

Recommended Start and Stop Points

North Side: Sopris Park (6,170 feet) on Seventh Street in Carbondale; 25.4 miles and 2,610 feet of elevation gain to McClure Pass. At the intersection of Colorado Highway 133 and Main Street, turn east onto Main and then turn right on Seventh Street. The park is near the Carbondale John M. Fleet Municipal Pool. If you're in historic downtown, you've gone too far; one block up Seventh is Sopris Park. It is a generous park with picnic tables, swing sets, and typical amenities such as rest rooms and a water fountain. It's a great starting point because it's close to everything.

South Side: Paonia State Park (6,735 feet) on Colorado Highway 133 at the north end of Paonia Reservoir 20 miles east of Paonia; 16.9 miles and 2,045 feet of elevation gain to McClure Pass. There is camping at two areas, Spruce and Hawsapple, but no water at either; the nearest water is at the Crystal Meadows Resort at the Kebler Pass road. There is also a picnic area 0.5 mile up a dirt road.

Alternate Start and Stop Points

North Side: Pullout (6,600 feet) on the left (east) side of Colorado Highway 133, 8.2 miles south of Carbondale; 16.8 miles and 2,180 feet of elevation gain to McClure Pass. There are several pullouts near here. This ample spot is used by fishermen because it is close to the Crystal River. It makes a good starting spot because it is shaded and cuts out the hotter, drier area around Carbondale, but sacrifices very little elevation gain.

Redstone (7,203 feet) on Colorado Highway 133, 16.4 miles south of Carbondale; 8.6 miles and 1,577 feet of elevation gain from the coke ovens to McClure Pass. Redstone is a small town restricted by the river and the canyon walls. Food, however, is unrestricted. Chicken and ribs, pies, breakfast, soups, sandwiches, and art are all for sale. A small public park is across the street from a blue and purple general store. The main road leads back north about 1 mile to Redstone Campground.

South Side: Downtown Paonia (5,698 feet), 1 mile off Colorado Highway 133 on Colorado Highway 187; 37 miles and 3,082 feet of elevation gain to McClure Pass. There seems to be a city ordinance against cars in this town: Every vehicle in Paonia is a dog-equipped pickup truck. Starting from Paonia makes McClure Pass a challenging ride. The town park is 0.3 mile east on Fourth Street.

National Forest sign (6,866 feet) on Colorado Highway 133, 29.3 miles east of Paonia; 7.7 miles and 1,914 feet of elevation gain to McClure Pass. This is about the spot where the trees stop and the sagebrush begins. There's not much here, but it's convenient and easy to see. McClure Campground, 2.5 miles closer to the pass, is supposed to have drinking water.

Road and Traffic Conditions

The road on the north side is excellent, and traffic is mellow because Colorado Highway 133 is not exactly a major artery. The south-side pavement is good to rough, with a few strips of crushed, gravelly pavement. Watch for rockfall down low where the road is cut deeply into the sides of short cliffs. At times, Highway 133 is quite narrow and gives the impression of a dirt road that was quickly paved without any extra engineering or expense. Traffic is light between Paonia State Park and Redstone, but there are several mines between Paonia State Park and Paonia, and these mean there are big trucks on a small road.

Descents

Both sides are short and fast, but end in valleys where most of the riding is on grades of 1 percent.

South Side: More varied because it starts off on a high plateau, but then follows the curves of East Muddy Creek. The south side doesn't have any curves.

North Side: Has one curve.

Sleep and Supplies

Even potable water is hard to come by on the west (south) side, which is not good because the area is hot and dry. There is plenty of everything in Carbondale and Redstone on the north side. On the south side, Paonia has almost everything; from the middle of downtown, you can find gun shops, flower shops, or health food stores. The Paonia bike store is really for kids' bikes, so unless you want to put coaster brakes on your machine, you'll have to go northeast to Aspen. For more information call the Carbondale Community Chamber of Commerce, 970-963-1890, for the north side; Paonia handles the south side, 970-527-3886.

The north side is in White River National Forest, 970-945-2521, within the Sopris Ranger District, 970-963-2266. The south side is in Gunnison National Forest, 970-874-6600, in the Paonia Ranger District, 970-527-4131. The Colorado State Parks, 970-921-5721, operates campsites near Paonia Reservoir. The useful campsites along Colorado Highway 133 on the north side are Janeway (no fee, but no water) and Redstone (the latter is reservable). There is dispersed camping available about 0.25 mile west of the top on the north side. There is only one Forest Service campsite on the south side, McClure Campground. The campsites at Paonia Reservoir State Park are well located; fee is $4 plus $5 if you have a vehicle, but despite this, there is no drinking water here.

MILEAGE LOG

★0   Sopris Park (6,170 feet), just behind the municipal pool off Main Street in Carbondale. Follow Main Street south.

0.3 Intersection with Colorado Highway 133. A strip-mall area in Carbondale can be used as a start if you want to avoid Sopris Park. Follow Highway 133.

2.2 Trout hatchery.

2.4 The road surface is poor, but there is a shoulder 6 to 12 inches wide.

3.2 Cross Pitkin County Line. Excellent views. Mount Sopris is off to the left, and ahead is a dark, wooded canyon headed by sharp, ice-bound peaks.

3.8 Sign says "Mount Sopris 12,959 feet." Pullout (possible starting place if you want to avoid Carbondale without sacrificing much mileage).

6.4 Grocery store, cabins.

8.3 Sign reads "No Camping within 0.25 mile of Crystal Road." A pullout immediately before the sign.

☆8.6 Large pullout (6,600 feet) on the left with ample, shaded parking.

11.5 Avalanche Creek Road 310 on the left. Turn east across the river to reach Janeway Campground about a quarter-mile up this dirt road.

11.8 Still gorgeous.

12.6 Large pullout on left.

15.3 North entrance to Redstone. This small road sticks close to the Crystal River on the way through town. It's a

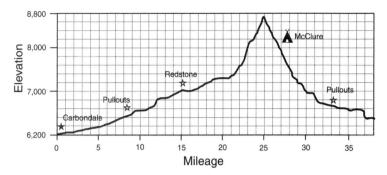

frontage-road extension of Redstone's Main Street. Redstone Campground is on the main road near here.

☆16.8 Redstone and its coke ovens (7,203 feet). A general store is across the street from a small public park. After Redstone, both the shoulder and the pavement improve.

20.0 Access to Placita Trail.

21.1 Extremely large pullout with historic plaques. A good place to start if you want to hit the climbing straight off.

21.9 Road to Marble. From here, things go up.

22.6 Series of fun curves.

23.0 Road is fairly straight and steep. Very fast downhill, but it is a wonderful climb because as you approach the top of the pass, many mountains, including Sopris, come into view.

▲25.4 McClure Pass (8,780 feet). Parking, pleasant aspens, a view of the Uncompahgre range.

25.7 Dispersed camping in an aspen grove on the left.

30.6 McClure Campground on the left. The road through here is great.

31.3 Road damage, giant dirt gap in the road.

☆33.1 Large pullout (6,866 feet) on the left near a "Leaving Gunnison National Forest" sign. The grade mellows here, and the road drops into sagebrush and along the river. This is a good alternate start/stop point or a good place to turn around for an out-and-back from the north side.

35.3 Intersection with Coal Bank road (dirt). Land is private.

39.7 The road is poor here, and the shoulder is worse.

★42.3 Paonia State Park (6,735 feet). A 0.5-mile dirt road leads to the camping area.

43.0 Road narrows, shoulder disappears, and the pavement gets worse.

45.6 Intersection with Kebler Pass road. Restaurant at Crystal Meadows Resort.

48.1 The road begins to look like a highway again.

52.4 Entering Somerset; small houses.

52.8 Portal Bar and Grill, Oxbow mining company. The road is narrow, and there is no shoulder through Somerset.

54.3 Intersection with road to Bowie.

61.5 Intersection with Colorado Highway 187. Turn south for downtown Paonia. Highway 187 becomes Grand Street.

62.2 Fourth and Grand, just past a gas station. To reach a huge city park, turn east on Fourth for 0.3 mile, past a couple of schools; the park is marked by a stout bronze statue of a miner, plus large ball fields and acres of space.

☆62.4 Downtown Paonia. From the middle of downtown, you can find gun shops, flower shops, and health food stores.

17 GRAND MESA
10,840 feet

Even though it's not technically a pass, this is still a hell of a hill. Only Mount Evans offers a bigger one-day gain. There are, arguably, the best aspens in the state along this road. The area isn't alpine, but here Colorado is making the transition to Utah, and Grand Mesa is an excellent refuge if the desert to the west is unusably hot. The proximity to Interstate 70 makes it easy to incorporate into many trips, and this road is definitely worth some time and a little detour. Though the road trends from southeast to northwest, here it is described as "east" and "west" for simplicity's sake.

EAST TO WEST: Distance from Cedaredge Town Park to I-70:
    51 miles
EAST SIDE: Distance from Cedaredge Town Park to high
    point: 19.6 miles
Elevation gain: 4,620 feet
Grades: Maximum 6%; average 3.4% for 3.3 miles, 4% for 5.1
    miles, 5.1% for 11 miles
Difficulty: 4
WEST SIDE: Distance from junction with Highway 330 to high
    point: 21.4 miles
Elevation gain: 5,640 feet
Grades: Maximum 6%; average 2.8% for 5.7 miles, 5.9% for
    15.4 miles
Difficulty: 5

Recommended Start and Stop Points

East (South) Side: Cedaredge Town Park (6,220 feet) on
West Main; 19.6 miles and 4,620 feet of elevation gain to the
high point. On Colorado Highway 65 at Main, there is a flashing caution light instead of a stoplight. Turn west here onto
West Main and go three blocks to Fifth to get to the park. This is
a fairly large park with plenty of parking all around, picnic
tables, and a rest room, but no water.

West (North) Side: Junction with Colorado Highway 330
(5,200 feet); 21.4 miles and 5,640 feet of elevation gain to the
high point. From Interstate 70, take exit 49 and go to Highway
65 south. Follow Highway 65 for 10 miles along the river. At
the junction with Highway 330, there are large open areas to
park. There are no other facilities, not even tables. This point
is easy to find and will maximize the hill climbing. Mesa is
1.9 miles up the road. There are a few restaurants in Mesa but
little public parking.

Alternate Start and Stop Points

East (South) Side: Junction with Old Table Mesa
Road/Forest Road 123 (8,736 feet), on the right side of Highway

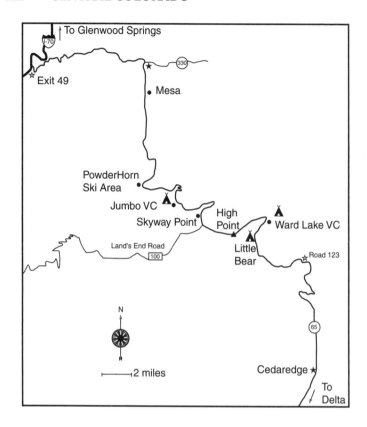

65, 10.5 miles from Cedaredge Town Park; 9.1 miles and 2,104 feet of elevation gain to the high point. There is nothing here except room for two cars to park, but it is a good halfway point if you'd like to ride farther down the north (west) side or just avoid the heat of the valley. The elevation is also cut about in half.

West (North) Side: Junction with Interstate 70 at exit 49 (4,787 feet); 31.4 miles and 6,053 feet of elevation gain to the high point. Just off the exit ramp are large dirt parking areas shaded by trees and protected by cliffs. There is a large sign detailing the virtues and attractions of scenic Highway 65. Starting here provides a 10-mile warm-up—and it will be warm—and an extra 413 feet of elevation gain, which puts the climbing over the 6,000-foot mark.

Road and Traffic Conditions

Colorado Highway 65 is mostly a scenic highway and, consequently, there is little industrial traffic. There is farm traffic low on the east (south) side, but most big vehicles on this road are pulling boats. Traffic is heavier on the west (north) side and can be erratic because drivers stop and start suddenly near scenic pullouts. The road surface is good on the east (south), but the top and west (north) side have a few nasty spots. The shoulder is best on the east (south) side also. Cattle guards are frequent and are not always signed. There is a big difference in climate between the west (north) and east (south) sides. The east (south) is ridable three seasons out of the year, but the west (north) is a summer and fall destination. Even a little snow on the west (north) side will blow across the road, making shadows a haven for thin ice.

Descents

West (North) Side: Tight curves, broken pavement, and slow cars dampen the descent. The road improves below just as the grade lets up. Still, anyone willing to push and pass cars will drop more than a mile in no time.

East (South) Side: Mellower but still brisk. The only thing to really watch out for is hitting cattle guards at 40 miles per hour. Unfortunately, the best shoulder is on the uphill lane.

Sleep and Supplies

On the east (south), Cedaredge has banks, stores, gas stations, and a museum all near the town park. The top of Grand Mesa is heavily developed with campsites, lodges, boating, biking, hiking, and other sporting facilities at Ward Lake Visitors Center, Skyway Point, and Jumbo Visitors Center. To the west (north) in Mesa, there are a few restaurants (pizza, beer, and Mexican food) but little public parking. For more information in the Cedaredge area, call the Delta area Chamber of Commerce, 970-874-8618. There is a separate chamber of commerce for the businesses on the Mesa, the Plateau Valley Chamber of Commerce, 970-487-9525. Farther afield from Mesa is the Grand Junction Chamber of Commerce, 970-242-3214.

There are many campsites along the road on the top of the Mesa; all are within Grand Mesa National Forest, 970-874-6600, Grand Junction Ranger District, 970-242-8211. There is no public camping down low because Grand Mesa National Forest is surrounded by private land, although there is a small private campground (Aspen Trails) about 3 miles north of Cedaredge on the east (south) side of the mesa, and you can sleep undisturbed at the intersection of I-70 and 65 on the west (north) side of the mesa. The campsites on top are Cobbett Lake, Ward Lake, Little Bear, Spruce Grove, and Jumbo.

MILEAGE LOG

★0   Cedaredge Town Park (6,220 feet), at Fifth and Main. Go east three blocks on Main.

0.25 Intersection with Colorado Highway 65. A bank is on the corner. Go north on the highway.

0.7 Small picnic area along the highway.

3.3 Aspen Trails private campground, with some cabins. Here you can stock up on ice cream and gifts.

5.9 The grade begins. Out across the Plains, way out, is the Sneffels range.

6.6 The shoulder is fine on the uphill, but small for the descent.

☆10.5 Road 123/Old Table Mesa Road (8,736 feet) on the right. There are three cattle guards through here, two of which are signed.

12.5 Entering Grand Mesa National Forest.

13.5 After 13.5 miles of shrub and piñon pine, you come into a forest with pines that are uncommonly large for Colorado.

14.0 The road is wavy and poor.

14.6 Ward Creek Reservoir turnoff on the right.

14.7 Top of the Mesa—but not the high point. The road flattens out here, but only temporarily. Pullout with rest rooms.

16.6 Main Visitors Center for Grand Mesa. Parking, toilets, fishing access, rangers, displays.

17.8 Grand Mesa Lodge, a motel and cabins, on Island Lake.

17.9 Road for Island Lake; camping, boating, fishing. The west (north) side of the mesa is more interesting.

▲ 19.6 High point (10,840 feet). Large pullout, skiers trailhead.

19.7 County Line. Things get cooler. Expect snow or ice in all but midsummer.

21.2 Land's End Road/Forest Road 100 on the left. Outhouses.

21.5 The road is bad through here; little if any shoulder and many rough asphalt patches.

22.2 View to the north.

22.3 Skyway Point, a great viewing area and a good place to stop before things go down in earnest.

22.8 Still no shoulder.

23.6 Cattle guard.

23.9 Pullout on the right.

24.0 The road quality improves, but there's still no shoulder.

25.6 Spruce Grove Campground. Water.

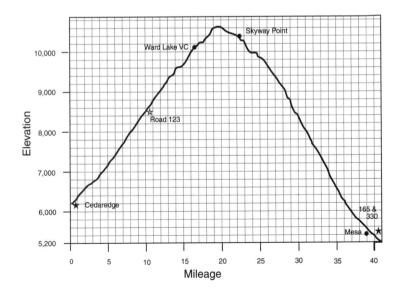

26.0 Mesa Lakes Resort. Food, lodging, fishing, hunting.

26.3 Jumbo Reservoir, Jumbo Ranger Station/Visitors Center, and Jumbo Campground. This is a most elaborate visitors' center. There's more information than you can use. Bike information is for mountain bikes.

27.0 The road is terrible; some sections are nearly dirt.

27.2 Overlook.

27.9 25 mph curves with much snow and/or sand.

29.3 Steep and curvaceous.

29.6 Road for Camp Kiwanis.

30.4 Cattle guard.

31.8 Powderhorn Ski Area.

33.2 The road is poor, but the shoulders finally open up.

33.4 Old Mesa Road.

39.1 Mesa, a small town with no central park and little public parking. The road from here to Highway 330 is steep.

★41.0 Junction with Colorado Highway 330 (5,200 feet). Large pullout. The road from here to I-70 is essentially flat, quite a contrast to riding on the mesa.

49.3 Large grassy area off the road is nicely shaded, a natural park.

☆51.0 Large parking area off I-70 (4,787 feet). Elaborate sign here describes Colorado Highway 65 and Grand Mesa.

SOUTH-CENTRAL COLORADO

18 UTE PASS
9,165 feet

Ute Pass is not exactly alpine. It is the only pass in the state with a stoplight on top. U.S. Highway 24 from Manitou Springs west to Woodland Park is laden with tourist attractions, and it is possible to start or stop from anywhere along the road and not be far from a Big Gulp. Ute Pass is also an unusual ride because the grade is so gentle near the summit but steep at the bottom on the east side. The longer you go, the easier it gets. The view of Pike's Peak, however, never quits.

EAST TO WEST: Distance from Manitou Springs to Florissant: 28.2 miles

EAST SIDE: Distance from Manitou Springs to Ute Pass: 20.3 miles

Elevation gain: 2,885 feet

Grades: Maximum 5.3%; average 3.3% for 5.5 miles, 3.4% for 2.8 miles, 4.8% for 1.7 miles

Difficulty: 3

WEST SIDE: Distance from Pullout East of Florissant to Ute Pass: 8.3 miles

Elevation gain: 1,005 feet

Grades: Maximum 2.5%; average 2.5% for 8 miles

Difficulty: 1

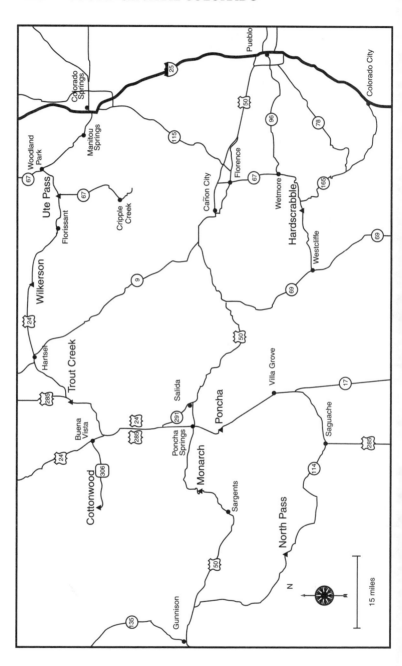

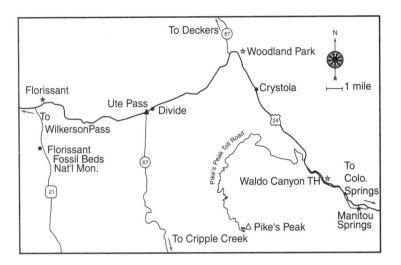

Recommended Start and Stop Points

East Side: Manitou Memorial Park (6,280 feet) on El Paso in the town of Manitou Springs on U.S. Highway 24; 20.3 miles and 2,885 feet of elevation gain to Ute Pass. In the summer Manitou Springs is a nonstop tourist swarm, and parking in town is a pain. At the corner of Manitou Avenue and El Paso, where there is an old narrow-gauge engine—the Pikes Peak Railway Manitou II—turn north on El Paso, which soon leads to Manitou Memorial Park and a howitzer. There is usually shaded parking back here, as well as water fountains, but no rest rooms. There is also some riverside parking 0.8 mile west of here just outside of town after an iron arch.

West Side: Large stone sign at a pullout (8,160 feet) on the right side of U.S. Highway 24, 0.3 mile east of Florissant; 7.6 miles and 1,005 feet of elevation gain to Ute Pass. The only public parking in Florissant is bar and restaurant parking. There is a town park 0.5 mile up a dirt road to the south, but is it uninspiring. The most reliable and easy to find parking area is near the town. The sign is farther from any stores, but other than that is the same as parking along the street in Florissant. The Florissant

National Monument is 2 miles down Teller County Road 21, and the monument is easy to incorporate into this trip, but to park there you must pay the entrance fee to visit the place.

Alternate Start and Stop Points

East Side: Waldo Canyon Trailhead (6,970 feet), a large parking area on the right (north) side of U.S. Highway 24, 3 miles west of Manitou Springs between miles 296 and 295, at a large Smokey the Bear sign; 17.4 miles and 2,195 feet of elevation gain to Ute Pass. The main advantage of starting here is getting out of city traffic without sacrificing much riding.

Woodland Park Visitors Center and Chamber of Commerce (8,396 feet) on U.S. Highway 24 at the intersection with Parkview in the town of Woodland Park; 7.3 miles and 769 feet of elevation gain to Ute Pass. There are a lot of possible starting points in and around Woodland Park. Traffic is intense on the weekends. The visitors' center, with water and rest rooms, is in the middle of town and close to everything. Just up U.S. Highway 24 is a rest area with picnic tables. At the intersection of Colorado Highway 67 and U.S. Highway 24, 1 mile east on the highway, a large shopping center has plenty of parking.

Road and Traffic Conditions

U.S. Highway 24 is wide enough to take the sting out of the traffic. The shoulder, however, is small until the Pikes Peak toll road, when things open up. Low down on the east side, rock walls hung with tree branches also encourage you to ride to the left. The pavement is excellent but gradually becomes ordinary on the west side. The shoulder lessens on the west side, and the road cuts through many tiny hills and rises. Grainy, decomposed Pikes Peak granite spills onto the road at each cut.

Descents

West Side: Going into a head wind down this side is more like climbing than descending. The road is not too steep, but it does roll over small hills, so there is no constant coasting.

East Side: Much faster, and there are a few appreciably steep sections just west of Manitou Springs. The lower 5 miles of the east side is the steepest section on this road, and the lower sections also have the best curves. Most passes save the curves and steeps for the top, but Ute is inverted.

Sleep and Supplies

Food and beverages are readily available in Manitou Springs (just west of Colorado Springs), Crystola, Woodland Park (grocery stores, shopping complexes; tourist facilities are dense here, so anything is available), Divide (liquor stores, gas stations), and Florissant. For more information on the area, contact the Manitou Springs Chamber of Commerce, 719-685-5089 or 800-642-2567, and the Ute Pass Triangle Chamber of Commerce, 800-780-9667, which has information covering a large area.

The area is in Pike National Forest, 719-545-8737.

MILEAGE LOG

★0   Manitou Memorial Park (6,280 feet) on El Paso. Head west on U.S. Highway 24.

☆2.9 Waldo Canyon Trailhead (6,970 feet) on the right. A Smokey the Bear sign marks the huge parking area. You can

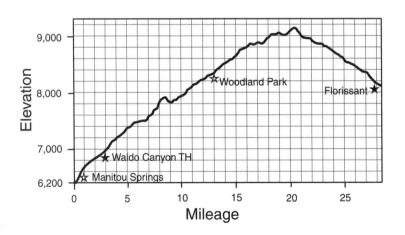

cross the divided highway here without going to another exit.

4.7 Pikes Peak Toll Road on the left. Shoulder improves. There are a couple of breaks in the grade, but overall it's a good, steady climb.

8.1 Top a rise; go down a bit.

9.8 Entering Crystola.

12.0 Shopping complex on the left. Possible alternate start.

12.4 Entering the town of Woodland Park.

☆13.0 Intersection with Parkview Road in Woodland Park; the Visitors Center and Chamber of Commerce (8,396 feet) is on the right. A rest area, complete with picnic tables and rest rooms, is a few blocks up on the left side of the road.

13.5 Intersection with Colorado Highway 67 north; large City Market and shopping center. Traffic is cramped and crowded, and the shoulder is minimal.

14.4 Road widens and improves. Good views of Pikes Peak to the south. Power lines and houses everywhere.

18.3 Large pullout on the right.

19.6 Entering Divide. Liquor stores, gas stations.

20.2 Intersection with Colorado Highway 67 south into Victor and Cripple Creek.

▲20.3 Ute Pass (9,165 feet). The pass is noisy, crowded, and treeless, but there's a good view out to the west. Ahead, the road is rolling but fairly flat.

24.3 Begin going down. U.S. Highway 24 begins to look like a mountain road. The shoulder is minimal, little more than 6 inches wide, and full of gravel and glass. Traffic is heavy.

26.2 Pullout on the left. There are many ranch estates.

★27.9 Large pullout (8,160 feet) on the right at a stone sign for Florissant, which is another 0.3 mile west. The sign looks like a tombstone for a town, but Florissant is behind, rather than under, the sign. There is some possible parking here, and the parking in Florissant is limited.

28.2 Intersection in Florissant with Teller County Road 21 leading 2 miles to Florissant Fossil Beds National Monument.

19 WILKERSON PASS
9,507 FEET

Wilkerson Pass is the division between Pikes Peak country and South Park. The east side is moderately steep, offering steady riding through low rounded hills, with Pikes Peak, a high rounded hill, off in the distance. The west side is mostly the long flats of South Park, with the Sawatch mountains off at an even greater distance. Wilkerson Pass has a wilderness feel because it is a woodland sandwiched between a more urbanized east and cattle lands to the west.

EAST TO WEST: Distance from Florissant to Hartsel: 30.4 miles
EAST SIDE: Distance from Florissant to Wilkerson Pass: 15.2 miles
Elevation gain: 1,347 feet
Grades: Maximum 5.9%; average 2.3% for 2.6 miles, 4.0% for 4 miles, 4.8% for 1.6 miles
Difficulty: 2
WEST SIDE: Distance from Hartsel to Wilkerson Pass: 15.2 miles
Elevation gain: 693 feet
Grades: Maximum 6.7%; average 6.7% for 1 mile, 3.0% for 2 miles
Difficulty: 1

Recommended Start and Stop Points
East Side: Intersection of U.S. Highway 24 and Teller County Road 21 in Florissant (8,160 feet); 15.2 miles and 1,347 feet of elevation gain to Wilkerson Pass. CR 21 leads 2 miles to Florissant Fossil Beds National Monument's visitors' center; to park there, you must pay the entrance fee. A visit to the monument is easy to incorporate into the trip up Wilkerson Pass. The only public parking in town is at bars and restaurants. There is also an

uninspiring town park 0.5 mile south on a dirt road. It's also possible to park at a large pullout on the right on U.S. Highway 24 at the large stone sign for Florissant 0.3 mile east of town.

West Side: Large pullout (8,814 feet) on the south side of U.S. Highway 24, 0.3 mile west of the intersection with Colorado Highway 9 in Hartsel; 15.2 miles and 693 feet of elevation gain to Wilkerson Pass. Hartsel, in the middle of South Park, has convenience stores, gifts, and a local bar, but the pullout west of town is the best spot to leave your car for any length of time.

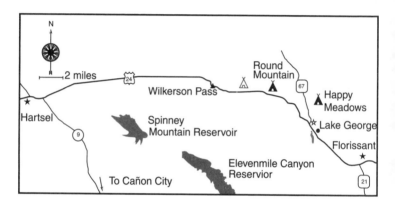

Alternate Start and Stop Points

East Side: Intersection with Tarryall Road/Park County Road 67, 5.7 miles west of Florissant, where there is enough room for a few cars (7,882 feet); 9.5 miles and 1,625 feet of elevation gain to Wilkerson Pass. From here the road wastes no time going up. The nearest place for food, water, and gas is 1.5 miles east in Lake George, but parking is difficult there.

Road and Traffic Conditions

U.S. Highway 24 is straight and goes over small hills instead of around them. The shoulder width and surface are adequate; near the summit, they are quite good. Traffic can be brisk, but it dies down west of Lake George because so many recreationists branch out from this point.

Descents

West Side: A short drop with long vistas.

East Side: Steep enough to keep your head down but your legs moving. The 10-mile descent can be faster yet with a tailwind because the road is well angled to catch north or west winds. There are no real curves or road hazards, so it's a good place to bear down and watch your speed increase.

Sleep and Supplies

Food and beverages are available in Florissant (see Ute Pass, ride 18), Lake George (liquor

The light grades and long views of Wilkerson Pass. Photo by C. Proenza.

stores, sporting goods stores), and Hartsel (gas stations, convenience stores, saloon/cafe, gift shop). There is no lodging west of Wilkerson until U.S. Highway 24 meets U.S. Highway 285 at Johnson Village west of Trout Creek Pass, but lodging increases exponentially to the east of Wilkerson. In the east, contact the Ute Triangle Chamber of Commerce, 800-780-9667; everything from Lake George westward is in Park County—call the South Park Chamber of Commerce, 303-836-4279.

The area is in Pike National Forest, 719-545-8737, and camping is within the South Park Ranger District, 719-836-2031. Dispersed camping is good near Wilkerson Pass. On the north side of the road about 2 miles below the summit is a web of Forest Service roads where shaded, flat, and relatively secluded campsites can be found. Established campgrounds are at Round

Mountain (water), just off a dirt road at mileage point 10.3, and Happy Meadows, 1.3 miles north on Tarryall Road/Park County Road 67 to the campground road, then another mile—there is no water here, but fishing is big. (More luxurious camping—hot showers, flush toilets—can be found 6 miles down CR 67 at Stagestop Campground.)

MILEAGE LOG

★0   Intersection of U.S. Highway 24 and Teller County Road 21 in Florissant (8,160 feet). Five miles of downhill ahead of you before you start to go up again at Lake George.

3.2 Gas station and Ponderosa Country Store.

3.6 RV campground on the left.

4.25 National Forest Service Work Center as you come into Lake George (7,900 feet), which has liquor stores and sporting goods stores, and which bristles with signs saying "no parking within ten feet of roadway."

5.25 Park County Road 90 (dirt); Spiny Mountain State Park is on the left.

☆5.7 Intersection with Tarryall Road/Park County Road 67 (7,882 feet) on the right. Happy Meadows Campground is about 2 miles north via CR 67.

9.4 Pullout on the left.

10.3 Road to Round Mountain Campground on the right (it's too far for bicyclists' use).

10.9 Intersection with County Road 31, the road to Tarryall Reservoir. Traffic gets light. The shoulder is fair with a mellow grade through rolling hills.

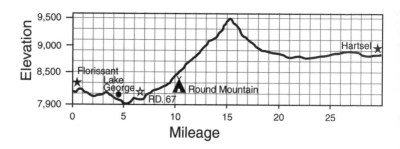

12.4 Pullout on the left. More trees, cooler temperatures here. Wilkerson Pass comes into view.

13.5 Road to the right. In the area, there is a large network of Forest Service and range access roads that lead to excellent dispersed campsites.

13.7 Rough road surface here.

▲ 15.2 Wilkerson Pass (9,507 feet). A little park, picnic tables, scenic overlooks out over South Park. You may or may not be able to get water here.

16.8 Leaving Pike National Forest. After 3 miles the road gets flat and rural. From the west, Wilkerson doesn't look like much.

30.0 Coming into Hartsel.

30.1 Intersection with Colorado Highway 9; continue straight on U.S. Highway 24.

30.3 Center of Hartsel (gas, saloon/cafe, gift shop).

★ 30.4 Large pullout (8,814 feet) on the left (south) side of U.S. Highway 24 just west of town—the best place to park.

20 TROUT CREEK PASS
9,487 feet

Trout Creek Pass is not so much a mountain pass as a valley pass. It simply divides the Arkansas River valley from the South Park Plateau. From the east, Trout Creek Pass is unimpressive, but the west side offers great, moderate riding and excellent views of the Collegiate Range. It is a prettier pass to descend than to climb, and this is especially so during sunrises or sunsets when even the mountains are dwarfed below clouds and dusty sunbeams. (Want to ride downhill to the top? Begin in Fairplay, which is higher than Trout Creek Pass by 482 feet. Fairplay is 21 miles north of Antero Junction.)

EAST TO WEST: Distance from Hartsel to Buena Vista: 28.4 miles

EAST SIDE: Distance from Hartsel to Trout Creek Pass:
   13.5 miles
Elevation gain: 626 feet
Grades: Maximum 4.4%; average 2.7% for 1.2 miles, 4.4% for
   1.6 miles
Difficulty: 1
WEST SIDE: Distance from Buena Vista to Trout Creek Pass:
   15 miles
Elevation gain: 1,549 feet
Grades: Maximum 4%; average 2.7% for 1 mile, 3.6% for 5.5
   miles, 4% for 1.7 miles
Difficulty: 2

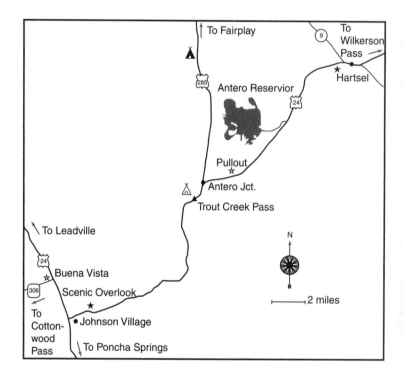

Recommended Start and Stop Points

East Side: First intersection of U.S. Highway 24 and
Colorado Highway 9 in Hartsel (8,861 feet), which sits in the

middle of South Park; 13.5 miles and 626 feet of elevation gain to Trout Creek Pass. There are convenience stores, gifts, and a local bar. One-third of a mile west on Highway 24 is a large pullout on the left (south) side of the road; this is the best spot to leave your car for any length of time. About a mile west is the second intersection of Highways 9 and 24.

West Side: Buena Vista Town Park (7,938 feet) at the corner of Highway 24 and Chaffee County Road 306; 15 miles and 1,549 feet of elevation gain to Trout Creek Pass. There is a Texaco station on the southeast corner of this intersection. The park has water and plenty of shaded parking and is surrounded by quiet streets.

Alternate Start and Stop Points

East Side: Park County Park (9,969 feet) at Fourth and Hathaway in Fairplay; 21 miles and 482 feet of elevation loss to Trout Creek Pass. Park at the park, next to the old brick library.

Pullout (9,064 feet) on the right side of U.S. Highway 24, 10.4 miles west of Hartsel; 3 miles and 423 feet of elevation gain to Trout Creek Pass. This option cuts out the flat of South Park, a good option for a moderate out-and-back of 36 miles to Buena Vista.

West Side: Scenic overlook (8,078 feet) on the right (north) side of U.S. Highway 24, 1.8 miles east of the junction with U.S. Highway 285; 10.7 miles and 1,409 feet of elevation gain to Trout Creek Pass. This option trims a bit of flat but leaves almost all the climbing. There are covered picnic tables and a good view of the Arkansas River valley below.

Road and Traffic Conditions

Traffic on the east side of Trout Creek Pass is so fast that even the motor homes make good time. The pass slows people down, but just before the summit, at Antero Junction, U.S. Highway 285 joins U.S. Highway 24, and because U.S. 285 is such a major road, expect heavy truck traffic. However, U.S. 285 is also large enough to have good shoulders and enough lanes. It is also well maintained and has a good surface.

Descents

West Side: It is a little unusual to crest a pass and begin with a moderate grade, but there is plenty of steep on the lower two-thirds of the ride.

East Side: The steepest part of the ride is just off the valley floor. There are several breaks in the grade, but the road is straight enough to make it fast if you work.

Sleep and Supplies

Hartsel has gas stations, convenience stores, a saloon/cafe, and a gift shop. There is nothing between Hartsel and Johnson Village south of Buena Vista on U.S. Highway 285. Antero Junction just before the summit is a ghost convenience store. This sad state of affairs is remedied with a vengeance at Johnson Village, which has lots of fast food. Buena Vista has gas stations, plenty of restaurants, convenience stores, and grocery stores. Fresh chain lube is only as far as Salida to the south. Hartsel is in Park County; for more information call the South Park Chamber of Commerce, 303-836-4279.

The east side is in Pike National Forest, 719-545-8737, within the South Park Ranger District, 719-836-2031. Right at the pass is the eastern boundary of the San Isabel National Forest, 719-545-8737. There are no established campgrounds in this area, but there is dispersed (and popular) camping just off the summit. The west side of the pass is checkered with private property, so you'll have to look carefully before camping along the road. There is a conveniently located KOA campground in Johnson Village.

MILEAGE LOG

★0   Intersection of U.S. Highway 24 and Colorado Highway 9 in Hartsel (8,861 feet). Go west on U.S. 24.

0.3 Pulloff on the left. This is the best parking point around Hartsel. The shoulder is as big as a lane.

1.1 Second intersection of U.S. Highway 24 and Colorado Highway 9. Sign says "Buena Vista, 27."

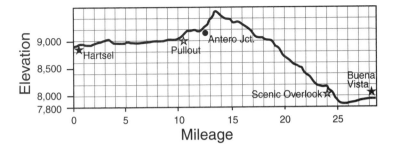

1.4 Good pullout.

4.7 Pullout near old building.

5.2 Road for Antero State Wildlife Area, a dirt road leading to a marsh.

☆10.4 Pullout (9,064 feet) on the right (alternate start/stop point). Here you begin heading up. There is no real shoulder.

12.57 Antero Junction, where U.S. Highway 285 comes in from the right (north) and immediately dumps a lot more traffic onto the road. Nothing here, but the quality and width of the road improve.

▲13.5 Trout Creek Pass (9,487 feet). Dirt road to the right heads to camping and Chubb Park, a trailhead to the midland bike trail. A pleasant area with no facilities, no posted camping restrictions.

14.5 Huge pullout. Good descent but not especially steep.

17.7 Intersection with Chaffee County Road 306. Bridge.

18.7 Mount Princeton and the Collegiate Peaks come into view.

20.5 Pullout on the left.

21.2 Road is excellent with an 18-inch shoulder, good views, and good cruising.

☆24.2 Large scenic overlook (8,078 feet) on the right (alternate start/stop point). Covered picnic tables overlook the valley.

25.3 Cross the Arkansas River.

25.4 Enter Johnson Village. KOA camping, much fast food, river rafting.

26.0 Junction where U.S. Highway 285 turns south and U.S.

Highway 24 turns north toward Buena Vista; go to the right.
★28.4 Intersection with Main Street in central Buena Vista
(7,938 feet). Excellent town park is just to the west at Chaffee
County Road 306.

21 COTTONWOOD PASS
12,126 feet

The sign welcoming you to Buena Vista reads "Now
this is Colorado." You can't help but think that while riding
Cottonwood Pass too. The road is flanked by fourteeners and is
thick with aspen. It has steep straightaways and beautiful
curves, and its elevation makes it Colorado's third-highest
paved road. This ride provides 4,173 feet of climbing in only
19 miles; unfortunately, only the east side is paved so there's no
description here of the west side. But the out-and-back from
Buena Vista to the top is one of the best rides in the state. As
with Mount Evans (ride 8), Trail Ridge Road (ride 3), and

A strong finish on Cottonwood Pass.

Independence Pass (ride 15), the road up Cottonwood is closed in winter.

ROUND TRIP: Distance from Buena Vista Town Park to
    Cottonwood Pass and back: 38.4 miles
EAST SIDE: Distance from Buena Vista Town Park to
    Cottonwood Pass: 19.2 miles
Elevation gain: 4,196 feet
Grades: Maximum 10%; average 2.2% for 5.3 miles, 2.5% for
    2.1 miles, 5.0% for 2.8 miles, 5.3% for 8.7 miles
Difficulty: 4

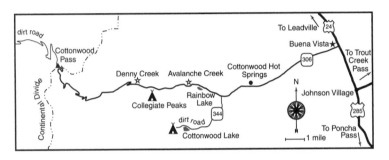

Recommended Start and Stop Points

East Side: Buena Vista Town Park (7,930 feet), at the corner of U.S. Highway 24 and Chaffee County Road 306 in Buena Vista; 19.2 miles and 4,196 feet of elevation gain to Cottonwood Pass. There is a hard-to-miss Texaco station on the southeast corner of this intersection. The great town park has water and plenty of shaded parking surrounded by quiet streets.

Alternate Start and Stop Points

East Side: Avalanche Creek Trailhead (9,365 feet) on the south side of CR 306, 9 miles west of U.S. Highway 24; 10.2 miles and 2,774 feet of elevation gain to Cottonwood Pass. There is a huge parking area here, but it is just a trailhead and has no facilities.

Denny Creek Trailhead (9,951 feet) on CR 306, 12 miles west of U.S. Highway 24; 7.2 miles and 2,175 feet of elevation gain to

Cottonwood Pass. The Denny Creek Trailhead is at the base of the 10-percent grade. This is an easy place to find because it is where the road is closed in winter, and there are many signs warning against travel in winter.

Road and Traffic Conditions

This road is just about ideal. There is little traffic because the west side is dirt, and the area is predominately residential and recreational so there's none of the agricultural traffic that is usually found on smaller roads. The road on the east side is fairly recently paved and, despite the elevation, does not have frost heaves and cracks. The shoulders are slim down low but there when needed, and because the road is not maintained in winter, the shoulders are not covered in wheel-spin–inducing gravel. Up higher, the curves are well banked, and because the road does not cut deeply into cliff walls, there is little, if any, rockfall or debris. The Cottonwood Pass road is not maintained from November 15 to June 15, so you can expect it to be closed anytime between those dates. If the weather has been good, you may find the road closed but perfectly ridable. This is a Chaffee County road, and the State Highway Department may not offer information on it.

Descent

East Side: Right off the summit, the turns blend beautifully into one another. Your bike tips with the road and seems to store energy to speed into the straightaway to tip and launch again. This road has a rhythm, and riding it down is the closest a bike comes to carving perfect turns in deep powder. You'll finish with the turns just in time for the short 10-percent-grade section, which gives a kick that lasts all the way into Buena Vista.

Sleep and Supplies

Buena Vista has plenty of restaurants, convenience stores, and grocery stores, and water can be had at the town park. Outside Buena Vista, everything becomes scarce. The nearest bike stores are in Salida to the south. There is plenty of lodging around

The top of Cottonwood Pass.

Buena Vista, and there is even the added attraction of Cottonwood Hot Springs (massage, mineral hot springs, hot tubs, cabins, rooms) and Mount Princeton Hot Springs. For more information, contact the Buena Vista Chamber of Commerce, 719-395-6612.

This area is in the San Isabel National Forest, 719-545-8737; the nearest ranger station is in Salida, 719-539-3591. The Collegiate Peaks Campground (free and unstaffed, as of this writing) is the only established campsite close to the road; it should have water. Dispersed camping can be had but is difficult to find above Collegiate Peaks because the valley is steep. A few miles south of the road is Cottonwood Lake Campground on County Road 344. The only camping in the valley floor is at the KOA campsite south of Buena Vista at the intersection of U.S. Highways 285 and 24 in Johnson Village.

MILEAGE LOG

★0   Buena Vista Town Park (7,930 feet) at the intersection of County Road 306 and U.S. Highway 24 in Buena Vista. Take CR 306 west.

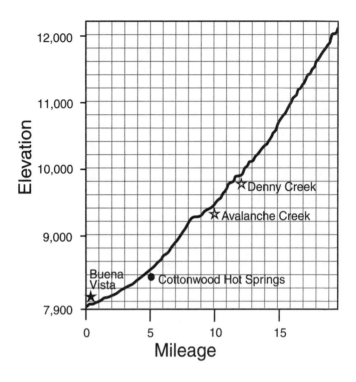

0.7 Mount Olivet Cemetery.

3.0 Drive-in theater.

4.3 San Isabel National Forest sign.

5.0 Begin curves.

5.3 Cottonwood Hot Springs on the right. The road is good here, but there is no shoulder. Here you enter the mountains from the valley floor.

6.0 Gentle curves and beautiful views.

6.8 Saddle Horse, a small townlike area. Spring Canyon Stables and Chaffee County Road 344 on the left; this is the road to Cottonwood Lake Campground, about 4 miles away.

7.9 Turnoff for Rainbow Lake Resort. Minimal shoulder.

☆9.0 Avalanche Creek Trailhead (9,365 feet) on the right. Huge parking area.

9.7 Grade steepens.

11.0 Collegiate Peaks Campground on the left.

☆12.0 Denny Creek Trailhead (9,951 feet) on the right. Rest rooms, plenty of parking. The easy stuff ends. The road shoots up like a wall past an assortment of warning signs, one of which reads "From November 1st until June 15 this road is not maintained." This is the 10% section; there is a good 1-foot shoulder on each side.

13.0 Parking areas on both sides of the road.

13.8 Chaffee County Road 346 on the left.

14.4 Ptarmigan Lake Trailhead on the left.

15.4 Series of 20 mph curves. You are now at 10,800 feet. The road is excellent, well banked, and generally clean.

18.0 The last portion of the road comes into view.

▲19.2 Cottonwood Pass (12,126 feet). There are stunning views to the west and, unfortunately, the road ahead is dirt.

25.9 On the return, 10-percent grade sign.

★38.4 Intersection with U.S. Highway 24 at Buena Vista Town Park in Buena Vista.

22 PONCHA PASS
9,019 feet

Poncha Pass is small but significant: It neatly divides northern from southern Colorado. For such a small pass, Poncha divides much: To the north are the Collegiate Peaks; to the west, the Arkansas watershed and all of northern Colorado; to the south, the Sangre de Cristos, the Rio Grande, and the San Luis Valley, with all its Southwestern character. The pass is fairly low and, consequently, hot, but cruising into the San Luis Valley down a light grade with the Sangre de Cristos in the distance should not be missed. The riding between Villa Grove and Saguache is definitely worthwhile, and even though the south side is not steep, it is long.

NORTH TO SOUTH: Distance from Poncha Springs to Saguache Town Park: 39.7 miles

NORTH SIDE:
   Distance from
   Poncha
   Springs to
   Poncha Pass:
   7.4 miles
Elevation gain:
   1,565 feet
Grades:
   Maximum 7%;
   average 3%
   for 3.1 miles,
   4.4% for 3
   miles, 5.8%
   for 1.2 miles
Difficulty: 2
SOUTH SIDE:
   Distance from
   Villa Grove to
   Poncha Pass:
   14 miles
Elevation gain:
   1,053 feet
Grades: Maximum 6.2%; 3% for 1 mile
Difficulty: 1

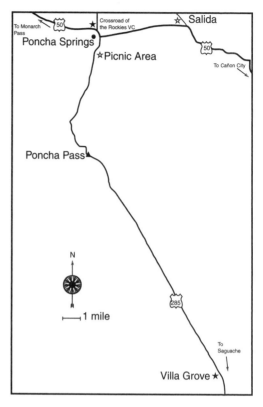

Recommended Start and Stop Points

North Side: Poncha Springs (7,454 feet), at the southern junction of U.S. Highways 50 and 285—the first one as you go west from Salida; 7.4 miles and 1,565 feet of elevation gain to Poncha Pass. Poncha Springs is one small burg, and this intersection is the center of it; it has a grassy patch of tree-shaded ground that serves well as a parking lot. There are many gas stations and restaurants within a quarter mile.

South Side: Villa Grove (7,966 feet) on U.S. Highway 285; 14 miles and 1,053 feet of elevation gain to Poncha Pass. Villa

The San Luis Valley.

Grove is a church, a house, and a grocery store that may not be open. There is no real place to park except along the road and traffic is fast. The alternate, Saguache, is preferable in many ways but more than doubles the distance, all of which is flat.

Alternate Start and Stop Points

North Side: Town Park (7,454 feet) on U.S. Highway 50 in Salida, 3.6 miles east of Poncha Springs; 11 miles and 1,565 feet of elevation gain to Poncha Pass). It is next to a public pool. There are picnic tables but no rest rooms; it is close to everything Salida has to offer. Because this is east of the main route, it isn't included in the mileage log.

South Side: Saguache Town Park (7,697 feet) on U.S. Highway 285 at Colorado Highway 114; 32.3 miles and 1,322 feet of elevation gain to Poncha Pass. This is a big park in a small town; there's no water but plenty of grass and shade. As an end point, Saguache is preferable to Villa Grove in many ways, even though it more than doubles the distance from the summit. The extra miles to Saguache are essentially flat because it is only 270 feet lower than Villa Grove.

Road and Traffic Conditions

The north side of Poncha Pass leaves plenty of room for both bikes and cars. The quality of the pavement is spotty. The south side is generally good; there are some stretches that have a huge shoulder, but on others the shoulder disappears entirely. The road is clean and not especially busy, but the south side is wide open and traffic is fast.

Descents

South Side: Poncha is not a fast pass. Wind makes the difference between fast cruising or tedium.

North Side: Quick because the road is fairly straight and short, and the grade is steady enough to keep you moving, especially near the bottom.

Sleep and Supplies

The north side has plenty, the south side has little. While in Salida or Poncha Springs, stock up on water, energy bars, or whatever else you can stuff into your jersey because you might not find any of that, not even water, until you get to Saguache or, if you're going straight south, Alamosa. Villa Grove, the first town south of the pass, has a grocery store that may not be open. For more information on the north side, contact the Heart of the Rockies Chamber of Commerce, 719-539-3591; to the south, contact the San Luis Valley Information Center, 719-852-0660.

U.S. Highway 285 threads its way through the San Isabel National Forest, 719-545-8737—the nearest ranger station is in Salida, 719-539-3591—and skirts the Rio Grande National Forest, 719-852-5941, barely touching either of them. Consequently, there is no dispersed camping or any established campgrounds along this road. There is camping at the O'Haver Lake area, but this is about 4 miles up a dirt road (Road 200, mile 5). There are also several private campgrounds around Salida.

MILEAGE LOG

★0   Junction of U.S. Highways 50 and 285 in Poncha Springs (7,454 feet) at a grassy patch of tree-shaded ground that can serve as a parking spot. Gas stations, restaurants within a quarter mile. Go south on U.S. 285.

0.3 Gas station and a good-sized parking area that is a usually busy mountain bike shuttle point; no shortage of water or power bars here.

0.9 Picnic area on the left and possible alternate start.

1.0 What had been a good road gets worse. The pavement on the shoulder is especially roughed up.

1.75 Intersection with County Road 115.

1.8 Grade steepens.

2.1 Leave the hot, dry country behind. The shoulder and pavement improves.

2.7 Pullout.

5.0 Intersection with County Road 200/Marshall Pass and Silver Creek Road, on the right.

5.2 Rainbow Trailhead on the right.

6.2 Aspens make this area cooler, woodsy.

▲7.4 Poncha Pass (9,019 feet). View of the Collegiate Peaks to the north and the San Luis Valley to the south. There is a short drop down the south side, then distance to be covered.

11.3 Good shoulder width, poor pavement, and a long, straight road.

★21.3 Villa Grove (7,966 feet). Grocery store, church, house. Nowhere to park except alongside the road. Traffic is fast.

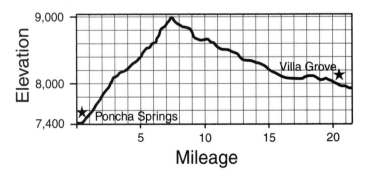

25.7 Junction with Colorado Highway 17 to the left (south), which goes to Alamosa. After here, the road shoulder becomes huge, and the road curves westward. Excellent surface, but the land all around is private for quite some time.

39.1 Enter Saguache.

39.4 Intersection with Colorado Highway 114 to the right (west).

☆39.7 Saguache Town Park (7,697 feet) at the intersection with Christy; here, U.S. Highway 285 is Eighth. This is a big park in a small town. No water but plenty of grass and shade.

23 MONARCH PASS
11,312 feet

Monarch Pass is a tough ride, especially from the east. If it were more than 12,000 feet, like Independence Pass or Trail Ridge Road, it would be brutal. Excellent engineering and modern construction have yielded smooth, steady grades on both sides. It is one of the steep passes that quickly puts deep, green valleys below you. U.S. Highway 50 is a good three-lane road, which makes it fast without being congested. Not surprisingly, passes near ski areas get a lot of rain and this is true of Monarch. The weather forms early here; in the afternoon, expect painful hail.

EAST TO WEST: Distance from Crossroads of the Rockies Visitors Center to Sargents: 27.2 miles

EAST SIDE: Distance from Crossroads of the Rockies Visitors Center to Monarch Pass: 17.9 miles

Elevation gain: 3,787 feet

Grades: Maximum 7.6%; average 2.2% for 7.1 miles, 4.2% for 3.4 miles, 6% for 6.9 miles

Difficulty: 4

WEST SIDE: Distance from Sargents to Monarch Pass: 9 miles

Elevation gain: 2,755 feet

Grades: Maximum 6.8%; average 5.9% for 8.8 miles
Difficulty: 3

Recommended Start and Stop Points

East Side: Crossroads of the Rockies Visitors Center (7,525 feet) on the east side of U.S. Highway 50 at the intersection with U.S. Highway 285 in Poncha Springs; 17.9 miles and 3,787 feet to Monarch Pass. This is about the smallest visitors center around, but that doesn't matter because there is a huge, unshaded parking area. It's easy to find, and its other virtue is a water hose located outside the building, which is useful before or after riding.

West Side: Sargents (8,557 feet) on U.S. Highway 50; 9 miles and 2,755 feet of elevation gain to Monarch Pass. This small town has everything from coffee to showers.

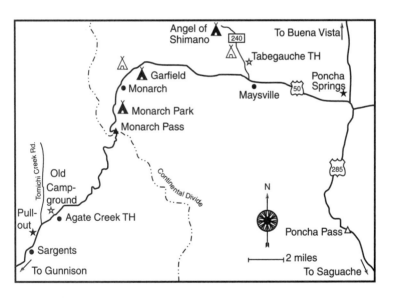

Alternate Start and Stop Points

East Side: Town Park (7,525 feet) on U.S. Highway 50 in Salida, 3.6 miles east of Poncha Springs; 21.5 miles and 3,787 feet of elevation gain to Monarch Pass. It is next to a public pool. There are picnic tables but no rest rooms; it is close to everything Salida has to offer. Because this is east of the main route, it's not included in the mileage log.

Tabegauche Trailhead (8,563 feet) 1.1 miles north on County Road 240, 6.1 miles west of the intersection of U.S. Highways 285 and 50; 12.9 miles and 2,749 feet of elevation gain to Monarch Pass. On U.S. 50, just after Maysville, CR 240 leads to the Angel of Shavano Campground and Picnic Area.

West Side: Pullout (8,600 feet) on the left (north) just before a bridge 1 mile east of Sargents, immediately before the grade begins; 8 miles and 3,700 feet of elevation gain to Monarch Pass. This is not an especially pleasant place to start—it's along the highway and unsheltered—but it is the best place to park if you want to ride the entire western grade. About another mile farther east is another pullout, at a sign for Gunnison National Forest, that can also be used.

Agate Creek trailhead (9,143 feet) on the right (south) about 3 miles east of Sargents; 7 miles and 2,169 feet of elevation gain to Monarch Pass. The road to the right is signed, and there is some parking here and some dispersed camping, but the area is small and cramped. About 50 feet before this area, on the left (north) side of the highway there is a large pullout and a stop sign at a road that leads to pleasant aspen groves and the abandoned fire rings of a defunct campground, which is much more pleasant and makes an excellent starting point. The area is close to the highway but still sheltered enough to feel private. There are no picnic tables or water. It is in Gunnison National Forest, so you can camp or park here at your leisure at no cost. This is much more enjoyable than parking along the road outside Sargents, but you'll sacrifice some riding.

Road and Traffic Conditions

U.S. Highway 50 is busy, but the road is big enough not to be crowded. Except for a short stretch on the east side, there are two lanes up and one lane down. Although there is enough shoulder width, you will probably be sharing a lane because the shoulders are much rougher and full of debris than the road. The surface is great the entire way on both sides of the pass, which makes it even more tempting to ride in the lane rather than the shoulder. There is a lot of truck traffic on U.S. 50. The most annoying type of traffic, however, is boats on trailers going to and from Blue Mesa Reservoir. Many boat-toters don't seem to realize how wide that trailer is.

Descents

Both Sides: Monarch is one of the faster passes. The road is smooth and the steep grade is constant. Catch a tailwind here and the bike's throttle will be stuck open. The curves are at best 30 to 40 miles per hour, so they spice up the descent without slowing it down. The smooth surface contributes to speed and is dangerously disarming because rough spots and divots crop up every now and then. It's likely that you'll have to pass and be passed, because cars go fast but trucks are slow.

Sleep and Supplies

The east side is well provisioned by Salida and Poncha Springs (many gas stations and restaurants). On the west side, Gunnison is a bit out of the way, but most essentials and even showers can be found in Sargents (gas stations, groceries, pop, beer, film, ice, café, bar, coffee, rest rooms). If you'd like a solid roof over your head, in Sargents, you can get a room and, more importantly, you can get a shower without renting a room—good news for the camping cyclist. The best camping on the west side is at the second alternate start, and there are established areas on the west side such as Garfield and the Angel of Shavano area. There are also several private camp-grounds around Salida. For more information on the Salida area, contact the Heart of the Rockies Chamber of Commerce at 719-852-5941; for information on west of the pass, call the Gunnison County Chamber at 970-641-1501.

The east side is in the San Isabel National Forest, 719-545-8737, Salida Ranger District, 719-539-3591. The west side is in the

Gunnison National Forest, 970-874-6600. There are also several private campgrounds around Salida.

MILEAGE LOG

★0   Crossroads of the Rockies Visitors Center (7,525 feet), on the east side of U.S Highway 50 at the intersection with U.S. Highway 285. Large parking area, water. This serves as a good starting point, although Salida 3.6 miles east (or the starting points for Poncha Pass, ride 22) can be used.

0.1 Pie and convenience stores.

5.7 Intersection with Chaffee County Road 220. The lower portion of U.S. 50 has a small shoulder, but the pavement is good the entire way.

5.9 Maysville, such a sleepy town that you may not get out without having an espresso. There is some lodging here, but nothing else.

☆6.1 County Road 240 (8,563 feet) on the right, leading to the Angel of Shavano Campground and Picnic Area. The Tabeguache trailhead, which makes a good alternate start, is 1.1 miles up this road. There is also good dispersed camping along this road between 1.4 and 1.9 miles from the highway. Private land is mixed with public land, so beware "no tres-passing" signs. The pavement ends after 3 miles; Angel of Shavano Campground and Picnic Area are 3.7 miles from the highway.

8.1 Large RV park and campground area.

9.4 Sign for San Isabel National Forest. Numerous pullouts before, at, and after the sign.

11.0 Large pullout and road on the right near a flashing sign indicating a 6-percent grade: "trucks stay in low gear." This road leads into the woods and branches out in many directions; there is good dispersed camping back here.

11.7 Small grocery store.

12.0 Monarch Lodge; rooms, rafting, jeep tours, fishing, biking, hiking. The restaurant here is not always open, but water and soda can be had. A lot of parking around here.

12.7 Road on the left for the Garfield Campground.

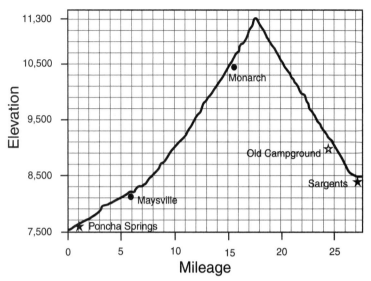

13.4 Road to a mine.

14.5 Monarch Park Campground on the left.

15.6 Monarch Ski Area on the right. This is tightly closed during the summer.

16.0 Only two lanes and poor shoulders here.

16.3 Old Monarch Pass Road on the right.

▲ 17.3 Monarch Pass (11,312 feet). Monarch's got it all: scenic chairlifts, a gift shop, a fast food place, a huge parking area, water, telephones, rest rooms. Nice views too, despite the kitsch.

21.4 Pullout on the left at a sign for Agate Creek Trailhead. A little parking here, but not much else; no good camping because the terrain is so steep.

24.2 Large pullout on the left.

☆24.4 Agate Creek Trailhead (9,143 feet) on the left (south). Some parking and some dispersed camping, but the area is small and cramped. About 50 feet past this, on the right (north), is a large pullout at a stop sign, which is much more pleasant and makes an excellent west-side starting point. The road leads through an aspen grove to defunct Agate Campground, with many small campsites. The area is close to the highway but still sheltered enough to feel private. There are no picnic tables, water, or anything else—just some abandoned fire grates.

25.3 Large pullout at a sign for Gunnison National Forest (can be used as a starting point from the west).

25.9 Leaving Gunnison County. The road gets worse.

26.0 Tomichi Creek Road on the right heads north, surrounded by private land.

☆26.2 Parking on the right just before the bridge (8,557 feet). This unsheltered area connected to the Daley Gulch area is the best place to park near Sargents.

26.3 Daley Gulch State Trust Wildlife Management parking area. An ugly, trashy area directly across the road from a large Highway Department complex.

★27.2 Sargents (8,557 feet); elevation high, population few. You can find a lot in Sargents, despite the fact that it's not much of a town: gas, groceries, pop, beer, film, ice, café, bar, coffee, rest rooms. You can also get a room and more importantly, you can get a shower here without a room—good news for the camping cyclist. There is no long-term public parking in town.

24 HARDSCRABBLE PASS
9,085 feet

Hardscrabble Pass is somewhat obscure because it doesn't go over a big range. It still has some good elevation gains and, like many smaller roads, is steeper than the big highways. The great pleasure of Hardscrabble is riding down into Wet Mountain Valley with the Sangre de Cristos towering in the west. The top of the pass is kind of a plateau, and the peaks emerge and submerge behind each small hill or row of aspens. This ride is definitely more scenic going from east to west than west to east.

EAST TO WEST: Distance from Wetmore to Westcliffe: 26.2 miles

EAST SIDE: Distance from Wetmore to Hardscrabble Pass: 16 miles

Elevation gain: 2,985 feet

Grades: Maximum 9%; average 3.8% for 7 miles, 4.5% for 3.4 miles, 8% for 1.8 miles

Difficulty: 3

WEST SIDE: Distance from Westcliffe to Hardscrabble Pass: 10 miles

Elevation gain: 1,197 feet

Grades: Maximum 6%; average 3.4% for 2 miles, 4.7% for 7.5 miles

Difficulty: 1

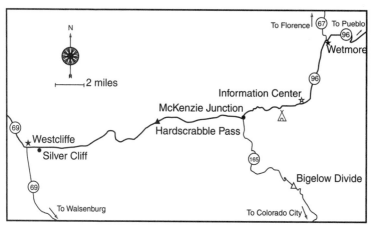

Recommended Start and Stop Points

East Side: Intersection of Colorado Highways 96 and 67 in Wetmore (6,100 feet), a small village 26 miles west of Pueblo; 16 miles and 2,985 feet of elevation gain to Hardscrabble Pass. A gravel parking lot here, across the street from Rena's Lone Pine Restaurant, makes a convenient parking area. Behind the restaurant, a road leads to the community center/library. Back here you'll find picnic tables, a barbecue grill, and wild plums.

West Side: Third and Main in downtown Westcliffe (7,888 feet); 10 miles and 1,197 feet of elevation gain to Hardscrabble Pass. Turn a few blocks south to reach the town park, which has water, rest rooms, and plenty of parking.

Alternate Start and Stop Points

East Side: Information center at a pullout (6,880 feet) on the right side of Colorado Highway 96, 4.6 miles west of Wetmore; 11.4 miles and 2,205 feet of elevation gain to Hardscrabble Pass. There is ample parking along with interpretive signs about the area's history and wildlife. Riding from here still leaves the steepest grades.

Road and Traffic Conditions

Colorado Highway 96 is more like a county road than a state highway. Traffic is light, but there are a few big trucks and the shoulder is generally small. The surface varies from fair to poor and is never bad enough to notice on the east side. On the west side, however, the road feels rough and cracked.

Descents

West Side: Wide open, with a light grade and a few dips and turns to keep it interesting. When you descend this side, sit up, take a drink, and enjoy the view.

East Side: It may be more scenic to ride from east to west, but it is a lot faster go from west to east. The east side's steepest grades are right in the sharpest curves. The canyon constantly pulls you down, testing nerve and balance. There is a respectable, nearly 4-percent grade all the way into Wetmore, so if you get tired going down, this is a good route.

Sleep and Supplies

Get your supplies in the towns at either end; this is a warm area in the summer, and there is no water along the road except from streams. Wetmore, in Custer County, is not large enough to have hotels, but there's Rena's Lone Pine Restaurant. Silver

Cliff, a Colorado mining legend, is smaller than Westcliffe but still has all the essentials. Westcliffe is a stockman's town with a few things to keep the tourists happy, and the tourist places stay open longer during the summer. The best way to get to know the area is to visit the giant map painted on a building near an ice cream parlor. For more information on the whole area, contact the Custer County Chamber, 719-783-9163.

This area is in the San Isabel National Forest, 719-545-8737, San Carlos Ranger District, 719-269-8500, though it is not in the San Isabel National Forest for long. Most of the ride is through private lands and there is little camping. There are two areas for dispersed camping at miles 6.1 and 6.6. There are established campgrounds along Colorado Highway 165 south, the road to Bigelow Divide, which is more than worth riding; the Ophir Creek Campground is about 12 miles south of McKenzie Junction.

MILEAGE LOG

★0   Junction of Colorado Highways 96 and 67 in Wetmore (6,100 feet). Small gravel parking lot across the street from Rena's Lone Pine Restaurant.

1.6 Greenwood Road to the left.

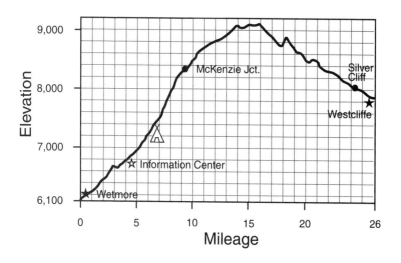

3.0 Lewis Creek Trailhead and National Forest access on a rough dirt road through private land.

☆4.6 Information center at a pullout (6,880 feet) on the right. A few interpretive signs about the history and wildlife of the area.

6.1 A good dispersed camping area on the left just before a mile marker. This is the most pleasant camping in the canyon.

6.6 More dispersed camping on the left. This area has been heavily used. It is sheltered from the road, but there's lots of burned wood and broken bottles.

7.8 Large shaded pullout on the right that is something of a trailhead. The grade picks up here at around 8 percent, and with good curves too.

8.0 Winding road; watch for gravel.

9.3 Pullout at a sign that says "Leaving San Isabel National Forest."

9.5 McKenzie Junction at the intersection with Colorado Highway 165. Highway 165 south, a fantastic road that is newly paved, leads to Bigelow Divide and Ophir Creek Campground.

10.4 Aspen stands and private lands.

12.0 The road flattens out.

13.0 The Sangre De Cristos come into view.

▲16.0 Hardscrabble Pass (9,085 feet).

17.7 Going up again through many curves. Interesting riding, but the road is a bit rough.

19.1 Bridge.

19.8 Silver Cliff city limit; the town is still a way off.

24.5 Silver Cliff, a Colorado mining legend; smaller than Westcliffe but still has all the essentials.

25.1 Silvercoin laundry and showers.

25.4 Country Store.

25.6 Westcliffe city limit.

25.9 T Intersection with Colorado Highway 69.

★26.2 Third and Main, downtown Westcliffe (7,888 feet). To reach the town park from here turn south for a few blocks, or from anywhere in town, head toward the steeple.

25 NORTH PASS
10,149 FEET

North Cochetopa Pass was part of the Santa Fe Trail, which was a pack trail linking Santa Fe and Missouri. It is now a little-used scenic highway called just North Pass. This road doesn't punch through a big range. It does its best to avoid mountains and stick close to rivers. Still, it's pretty hard to avoid steep grades near the Continental Divide, and North Pass is deceptively steep on the east side. The road looks flat because it travels through wide-open, rolling hills, but the grade is there like an unfelt wind. On the west side, the Cochetopa Canyon is a pleasant surprise etched into otherwise uneventful rangeland. Cochetopa Canyon isn't deep, but West Pass Creek has cut steep, pink granite walls that shade the road's constant turns. The 5-mile-long canyon is dotted with small campsites and picnic areas, each one as pleasant as the next.

EAST TO WEST: Distance from Saguache Town Park to U.S. Highway 50: 61 miles
EAST SIDE: Distance from recommended pullout to North Pass: 16 miles
Elevation gain: 2,008 feet
Grades: Maximum 7%; average 3.7% for 1.3 miles, 4.9% for 5.5 miles
Difficulty: 3
WEST SIDE: Distance from BLM Campground to North Pass: 13.5 miles
Elevation gain: 1,387 feet
Grades: Maximum 7.5%; 6.6% for 1.7 miles
Difficulty: 2

Recommended Start and Stop Points
East Side: Pullout (8,141 feet) on Colorado Highway 114 halfway between miles 48 and 47, 14.2 miles west of Saguache. This spot is not heartily recommended, but it is the best place to

start if you want to avoid the hot, flat, badly broken stretch just out of Saguache. Here the land changes from sage and field to trees and hills.

West Side: BLM Campground (8,762 feet) on Colorado Highway 114, 17.3 miles east of the intersection with U.S. Highway 50; 13.5 miles and 1,387 feet of elevation gain to North Pass. This campground is the southernmost of a series of picnic areas and campgrounds in the Cochetopa Canyon. If you are traveling north, the area is just at the mouth of a canyon of pink rock. There are outhouses, campsites, and, at least so far, no signs asking for money. There is, however, no water here except for the creek.

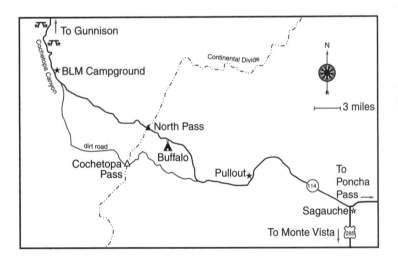

Alternate Start and Stop Points

East Side: Saguache Town Park (7,700 feet) at the intersection of Eighth and Christy, eight blocks south of U.S. Highway 285; 30.2 miles and 2,449 feet of elevation gain to North Pass. Saguache is a small town, so everything—the school, church, museum, and sheriff—are all in walking distance. There's no water at the park but plenty of shade and grass. This is as good a place as any to ride to North Pass. The only disadvantage of starting here is that the road just outside of town is bad, hot, and flat.

West Side: There are several other picnic and camping spots every few miles for about five miles downstream of the recommended site. These are not much different from the recommended area. There are outhouses, but the only water is what's in the creek.

Road and Traffic Conditions

West of Saguache, Colorado Highway 114 is terrible, rough, and so narrow that weeds and grass are eating through the white line. The road surface varies from okay to bad. The upside is lots and lots of towering sunflowers. The road improves as you approach the pass, however, and by the time you reach the Rio Grande National Forest you'll be on a smooth, wide shoulder. The west side is consistently narrow but in good shape. Traffic is light and local.

Descents

West Side: The way down is fairly steep and there are a few curves, but the descent is over almost before it starts; after about five minutes you're back in rangeland. After the steep section, the road gets much worse. Cochetopa Canyon is winding and cool, but never steep.

East Side: Riding east on Highway 114 is the most pleasant and beautiful way to descend into the San Luis Valley. After the initial drop, the terrain is rolling but always steep enough to keep you moving easily, and the landscape changes from forest to rangeland as the view of the valley opens before you.

Sleep and Supplies

There is enough water along Colorado Highway 114, but that doesn't mean there is a lot of it, and during the summer, you'll need a lot of it. This road is in the middle of the state, but it seems far from everything. In the small town of Saguache, everything is in walking distance. The Gunnison area is the closest thing on the west side of the pass. For more information on the San Luis Valley, call the San Luis Valley Information Center, 719-852-0660; for the Gunnison area, call the Gunnison County Chamber, 970-641-1501.

The first 25 miles are along private land, but the rest of the way is in Rio Grande National Forest, 719-852-5941, Saguache Ranger District, 719-655-2547. Buffalo Pass Campground is near the summit. A BLM camp is at the mouth of Cochetopa Canyon, and other campsites are scattered a few miles into the canyon.

MILEAGE LOG

☆0   Saguache Town Park (7,700 feet) at Eighth and Christy. Plenty of grass and shade but no water. Go three blocks north on Eighth.

0.2 Intersection of U.S. Highway 285 and Colorado Highway 114. There are a few mud-brick buildings and log cabins. Take Highway 114 west.

0.7 Forest Service Ranger Station. Parking, water, brochures.

0.9 By now Highway 114 is a narrow road through wide-open country.

4.0 Rough road. Pickup trucks tow horse trailers and recreational vehicles tow cars.

8.4 Pullout on the right. The land all around is private.

13.5 Pullout on the right. Low, flat hills, piles of hay, and short cliffs begin to appear.

★14.2 Good pullout (8,141 feet) on the right; this is the recommended start/stop point because here things cool down, the road gets better, trees appear, and the road starts going up.

14.9 Sign for Big Springs Picnic Area, 5 miles down a dirt road.

21.1 Dirt road on the left leads to South Cochetopa Pass.

22.2 Interesting rock formations.

24.9 Spanish Creek and Sheep Creek Road on the right. This is a neat area on BLM land. The pavement is excellent with a 2-foot shoulder.

25.6 Huge pullout just behind a sign "Entering Rio Grande National Forest." This is large enough to be a good alternate start.

26.2 Road to Buffalo Pass Campground on the left. This extensive campsite is 0.5 mile down the dirt road. Dispersed camping can be had nearby. Near the road there is a water spigot posted as potable. Highway 114 is excellent from here to the pass.

28.5 Pullout.

▲ 30.2 North Pass (10,149 feet). No rest areas or big signs here, just a road.

35.4 Forest Service access road for Archuleta Creek on the left.

37.7 The road is chip and dip—very rough—through here.

40.6 Wide-open park and low hills.

41.0 Forest Service Road 14 on the left.

★ 43.7 Entering Cochetopa Canyon. On the right is a BLM camping area (8,762 feet). No fee, or at least no sign requesting one. This is a beautiful little area alongside West Pass Creek right at the mouth of the canyon. Cochetopa Canyon isn't deep, but the creek has cut steep, pink granite walls that shade the constant turns. The canyon is 5 miles long and dotted with small campsites and picnic areas, each one as pleasant as the next.

45.0 Small parking area, access to the creek and shade.

46.4 Camping and picnic spot.

46.6 Picnic area on the right.

47.9 Picnic area on the left.

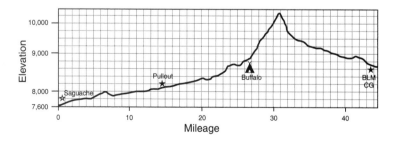

48.5 The road gets rough; the shoulder disappears. Leave the canyon and enter the range.

53.2 Gunnison County Line.

53.7 Many curves. The road still follows the meanderings of the creek. Nearby land is private and occupied by cows.

61.0 Intersection with U.S. Highway 50. Gunnison, about 7 miles to the west, is the nearest town with any facilities.

SOUTHERN COLORADO

26 CUCHARAS PASS
9,941 FEET

Colorado Highway 12 forms a giant horseshoe around the Spanish Peaks, so it doesn't have a lot of high speed, got-to-get-there traffic. What it does have is beauty and variety at every turn. The ride begins in La Veta, from where you can go up either Cucharas Pass or North La Veta Pass (ride 27). The north side of Cucharas Pass starts by dodging through volcanic dikes and rising above a cool, shadowed forest. The summit has broad fields of aspen below looming peaks, and the south side drops fast into rolling green hills and dry lands. The north side of this pass is much more convenient than the south side; a 34.4-mile out-and-back from La Veta is a great option.

NORTH TO SOUTH: Distance from La Veta to Stonewall: 32.1 miles
NORTH SIDE: Distance from La Veta to Cucharas Pass: 17.2 miles
Elevation gain: 2,932 feet
Grades: Maximum 7.5%; average 2.2% for 8.6 miles, 4.2% for 5 miles, 6.1% for 2.5 miles
Difficulty: 3
SOUTH SIDE: Distance from North Lake to Cucharas Pass: 7.5 miles
Elevation gain: 1,316 feet
Grades: Maximum 8%; average 4.2% for 4.2 miles, 8% for 1.2 miles
Difficulty: 2

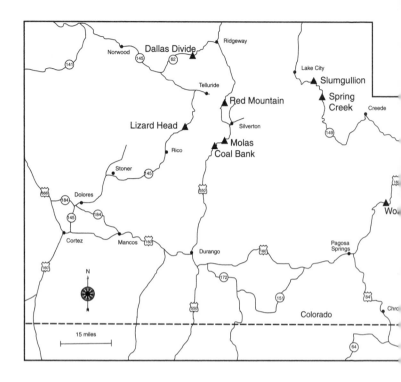

Recommended Start and Stop Points

North Side: Colorado Highway 12/Main Street at the railroad tracks in La Veta (7,009 feet); 17.2 miles and 2,932 feet of elevation gain to Cucharas Pass. To reach the La Veta town park, from the north on Highway 12, turn right on Ryus Street soon after crossing a series of railroad tracks. The park is close to groceries, gas, and restaurants. Head south on Highway 12 and the road soon gets beautiful, sandwiched between volcanic dikes and a meandering stream.

South Side: North Lake Picnic Area (8,625 feet) on the right on Colorado Highway 12, 7.4 miles north of Stonewall; 7.5 miles and 1,316 feet of elevation gain to Cucharas Pass. North Lake is a state wildlife area and a popular fishing spot equipped with the fisherman in mind: rest rooms, picnic tables, etc. There is no water here, except for the lake. This is the last public land on the south side of Cucharas Pass.

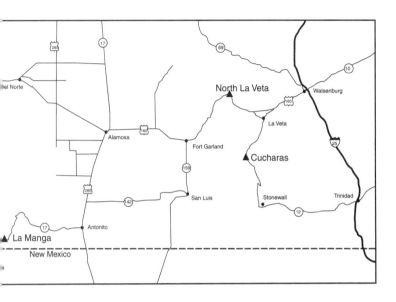

A late autumn morning on Cucharas Pass.

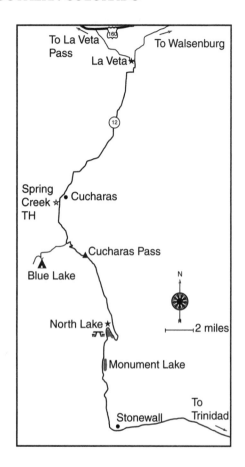

Alternate Start and Stop Points

North Side: Main Street in the town of Cucharas (8,456 feet); 5.9 miles and 1,485 feet of elevation gain to Cucharas Pass. Cucharas is a concentrated mountain town (gifts, T-shirts, liquor, barbecue fishing licenses, hunting supplies, cigarettes, antiques, fudge, mountain furniture) squeezed into a valley, so there's not much extra parking. The best place to park is at the Spring Creek Trailhead, a Forest Service day-use fee area (picnic tables, rest rooms) 0.6 mile south of town.

South Side: Stonewall (7,750 feet) on Colorado Highway 12, 31 miles east of Interstate 25 at Trinidad; 14.9 miles and 2,190 feet of elevation gain to Cucharas Pass. This is the best alternate start/stop point on the south side because the grade quits for good here, and it is a good distance from the summit. There are no public areas and not even anything that might be considered a pullout. The only place to park is on the highway shoulder.

Road and Traffic Conditions

The shoulder is slim the whole way, but so is the traffic. There is some tourist and ranch traffic, but because Colorado Highway 12 is hardly a major thoroughfare, there are few trucks or motor homes. The road isn't etched into a steep mountainside and there aren't a lot of side roads, so the surface is cleaner than most highways. If this weren't enough, it's even smooth, though it gets rougher near Stonewall and stays that way to Trinidad to the east. This is a great ride anytime except winter, but the north side might surprise you with snow or ice in spring or autumn.

Descents

South Side: Steep off the summit. The road drops, levels off for a short bit, and then drops steeply again. This series of steps is a high-speed blast, and chances are you'll have the road to yourself.

North Side: The south side has the best riding, but the north side has the best curves.

Sleep and Supplies

Among La Veta (groceries, gas stations, restaurants), Cucharas, and Stonewall (general store, cabins, RV camping), the necessities are never far away. Cucharas has a big supply of gifts, T-shirts, liquor, barbecue, fishing licenses, hunting supplies, cigarettes, antiques, fudge, and mountain furniture—not that you could carry this stuff on your bike. You can't buy bikes or bike stuff around here, but you can get everything else. For more information, contact the La Veta–Cucharas Chamber of Commerce, 719-742-3676, or, to the southeast, the Trinidad–Las Animas County Chamber, 719-846-9285.

The area is in the San Isabel National Forest, 719-486-0749, San Carlos Ranger District, 719-269-8500. Camping is difficult. Most of the land right along the road is private, so dispersed camping is not an option. There are good Forest Service sites up the Blue Lakes road, but that road is dirt and the sites are several miles from Colorado Highway 12.

MILEAGE LOG

★0   Colorado Highway 12 (Main Street) at the railroad tracks in La Veta (7,009 feet). As you come into town from the north, just after the railroad tracks turn right onto Ryus Street to reach the excellent town park. To begin the ride, from Highway 12 at the railroad tracks, take the highway south.

0.5 A few sharp curves.

8.1 Cross Cucharas River.

☆11.3 Intersection with Main Street in Cucharas (8,456 feet). Gifts, T-shirts, liquor, barbecue, fishing licenses, mountain furniture, fudge, cigarettes, hunting supplies, antiques.

11.9 Spring Creek Trailhead on the right. This good alternate start/stop point has picnic tables and rest rooms.

12.3 Enter the San Isabel National Forest.

13.3 Road to Cucharas Ski Area on the right. Cucharas Mountain Resort and scenic chairlift.

14.9 Blue Lake Road on the right. Sharp curve with parking and rest rooms. Good Forest Service campgrounds a few miles up this dirt road.

▲17.2 Cucharas Pass (9,941 feet). A small place to pull over, a

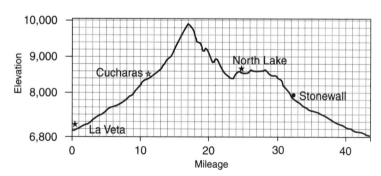

cattle pen, and Forest Road 46 to Cordova Pass. Colorado Highway 12 is good all the way down, with very little traffic and a slim shoulder.

23.3 Intersection with County Road 213 on the left.

23.9 North Lake Dam.

★24.7 Big pullout on the right at North Lake Picnic Area (8,625 feet). Rest rooms, picnic tables.

25.7 Intersection with Forest Road 34.5. No camping next 4 miles. Day use only. You could park here if the North Lake area is full.

27.9 Monument Lake on the left, a small lake with a monolithic stone jutting out of the middle of it. The area is dominated by the Monument Lake Resort.

☆32.1 Stonewall (7,750 feet). There is little here and no public parking. After Stonewall the road is permanently flat.

27 NORTH LA VETA PASS
9,413 FEET

North La Veta Pass has a practical feel. It's more of a way to get somewhere than a destination. The road is straight, not too steep, and not too spectacular, although near the bottom of the west side you travel under the Blanca/Little Bear massif. From the start/stop point of La Veta, you can go up either North La Veta or Cucharas Pass (ride 26). The east side gains nearly 2,500 feet, and it is always a pleasure to descend west into the San Luis Valley. Because the grades are not particularly steep, the weather affects the difficulty of this ride more than most other passes. The wind makes for a fast ascent or a grudging, frustrating ride down. Colorado Highway 159 south into San Luis is also an excellent road if you want to add some flat distance onto the ride.

EAST TO WEST: Distance from La Veta Town Park to Fort Garland Museum and Visitors Center: 33.7 miles

EAST SIDE: Distance from La Veta Town Park to North La
    Veta Pass: 13.6 miles
Elevation gain: 2,474 feet
Grades: Maximum 7.2%; average 3.0% for 10.5 miles, 4.2% for
    1 mile, 7.2% for 1.5 miles
Difficulty: 2
WEST SIDE: Distance from Fort Garland Museum and Visitors
    Center to North La Veta Pass: 20.1 miles
Elevation gain: 1,538 feet
Grades: Maximum 4.6%; average 2.8% for 4.4 miles, 3.8% for
    1.7 miles
Difficulty: 2

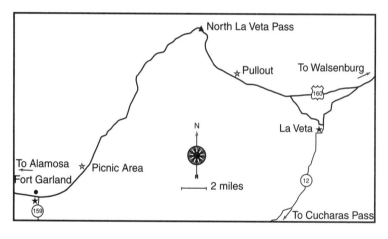

Recommended Start and Stop Points

East Side: La Veta Town Park on Ryus Street in La Veta
(7,009 feet); 13.56 miles and 2,474 feet of elevation gain to North La
Veta Pass. Coming into town from the north on Colorado Highway
12, soon after crossing a series of railroad tracks turn right on Ryus
Street. The park is close to groceries, gas, and a restaurant.

West Side: Fort Garland Museum and Visitors Center
(7,875 feet) on Colorado Highway 159, 0.2 mile south of U.S.
Highway 160; 20.1 miles and 1,538 feet of elevation gain to
North La Veta Pass. The museum offers an interesting slice of
life long gone by. There is an extensive regional and Colorado

Rain closing in on La Veta Pass.

book store and a few bullets under glass; plus ample parking, rest rooms, water, and nearby food.

Alternate Start and Stop Points

East Side: Pullout at Veteran's Memorial (8,144 feet) on the north side of U.S. Highway 160, 8.5 miles west of La Veta and 0.7 mile east of mile 283; 5.1 miles and 1,269 feet of elevation gain to North La Veta Pass. This is a good place to cut the elevation in half, but there is nothing here besides the memorial.

West Side: Picnic area (8,131 feet) on U.S. Highway 160, 3.9 miles east of the intersection with Colorado Highway 159 in Fort Garland; 16 miles and 1,282 feet of elevation gain to North La Veta Pass. This picnic area is in the middle of nowhere; it is surprising to see, but it can be useful and has a good view of Blanca and Little Bear. There are picnic tables and a tin roof, which is a nice thought but slim shelter. There are no rest rooms or water.

Road and Traffic Conditions

U.S. Highway 160 is the major eastern route into the San Luis valley, so expect a lot of traffic and trucks of every variety. Traffic isn't too fast, however, and the road is always wide enough for bikes. The road surface is fair. It is two lanes up, one down. When the road doesn't have three lanes, the shoulder is plenty big, and because it is a heavily used road, it is well maintained. There is some grunge and trash off the road, but generally the shoulder is as good as the traffic lanes, which makes the traffic much easier to ignore.

Descents

North La Veta Pass doesn't give away much speed. Both sides are straight and smooth, but even so, you'll have to work to make great time. On North La Veta, you can almost go fast in either direction and the thing that will decide it is wind.

West Side: The San Luis Valley heats up early, and the rising warm air makes a westerly wind sooner than most places.

East Side: With a steady 3-percent grade, you don't have to work as hard.

Sleep and Supplies

In La Veta you'll find groceries, gas stations, and restaurants. Fort Garland has a small grocery store, a few convenience stores, and some cafes. For more information on the east side, contact the La Veta–Cucharas Chamber of Commerce, 719-742-3676; west of the pass, contact the San Luis Valley Information Center, 719-862-0660, or for the area around Fort Garland, the San Luis Chamber, 719-672-3355.

This road touches some public land, but nothing useful. You won't find camping along this road.

MILEAGE LOG

★0   La Veta Town Park (7,009 feet) on Ryus Street. To pick up U.S. Highway 160 without backtracking through town, head west on Ryus.

0.1 Small bridge. Stay on this road as it weaves through farmland for 3.7 miles.

3.8 Intersection with U.S. Highway 160. Turn left. The road surface is fair and wide enough. It is two lanes up, one down and gets a lot of traffic of every variety.

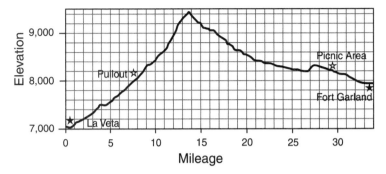

7.2 Sign says "summit, 8 miles." The road is good and nearly flat.

☆8.5 Large pullout (8,144 feet) on the right for a memorial to veterans killed in Italy during World War II. Parking, but no other facilities.

10.4 Good pullout.

▲13.6 North La Veta Pass (9,413 feet). La Veta is uncelebrated. Nothing here but a few road signs and a good shoulder.

15.3 Road to Paradise Acres on the right.

27.5 Come out of the mountains and into the San Luis Valley. Nothing between the top of the pass and Fort Garland. The Little Bear/Blanca massif dominates the northern view and it's all valley to the south.

☆29.6 Picnic area (8,131 feet) on the right in the middle of nowhere. Two shaded picnic tables off the side of the road; no water. This a good alternate start/stop point.

31.7 Intersection with the Forbes-Cucharas road on the left. The shoulder is big.

33.0 Entering the town of Fort Garland.

33.5 Intersection with Colorado Highway 159. A small grocery, a few convenience stores, some cafes. Turn left (south) onto Highway 159 for the Fort Garland Museum.

★33.7 Fort Garland Museum and Visitors Center (7,875 feet); plenty of parking and nearby food as well as water and rest rooms.

28 SLUMGULLION and SPRING CREEK PASSES
11,530 feet and 10,901 feet

Slumgullion and Spring Creek Passes are not as difficult as the numbers make them appear, though to ride the entire distance from Lake City to South Fork is a long haul. There are many options for a shorter ride, especially on the south side. Even though you know you're in the high mountains, the expected rugged peaks and twisty roads never appear. Near the summit, dense woods make the road a dark corridor, but an occasional break in the woods creates a window to distant peaks. Slumgullion is one of the steeper passes in the state, but for some reason it's more fun than relentless, just under 11 miles from the start in Lake City. The plateau between the two passes is only 6.5 miles, and from Spring Creek Pass southeast down the Rio Grande valley, the road just moseys along at the same lazy pace as the river. Together, Spring Creek and Slumgullion provide excellent variety on good roads with little traffic and cool weather. Ask for more and you won't get it.

NORTH TO SOUTH: Distance from Lake City to Silverthread Visitors Center: 75 miles

NORTH SIDE: Distance from Lake City to Slumgullion Pass: 10.4 miles; to Spring Creek Pass, 17 miles

Elevation gain: To Slumgullion Pass, 2,872 feet; to Spring Creek Pass, net 2,265 feet, total 3,380 feet

Grades: Maximum 9%; average 7.0% for 7.2 miles (up), 4.5% for 4.7 (down), 5.1% for 1.7 miles (up to Spring Creek)

Difficulty: 3

SOUTH SIDE: Distance from Spring Creek Reservoir Picnic Ground to Spring Creek Pass: 12.3 miles; to Slumgullion Pass, 19 miles

Elevations: To Spring Creek Pass, 1,649 feet; to Slumgullion Pass, 2,278 feet net, 3,415 feet total

Grades: Maximum 5.4%; average 2.6% for 6.2 miles, 4% for
    5 miles, 4.7% for 4.3 miles, 5.1% for 1 mile, 5.3% for 1.6
    miles, 5.1% for 1.7 miles (down), 4.5% for 4.7 miles (up
    to Slumgullion)
Difficulty: 3

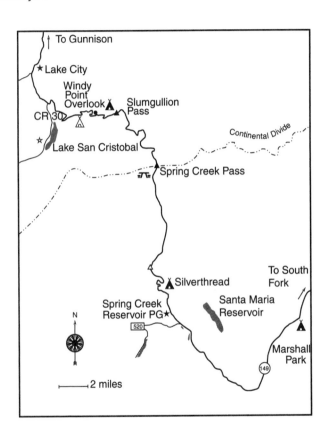

Recommended Start and Stop Points

North Side: Intersection of Second and Gunnison in Lake
City (8,658 feet); 10.4 miles and 2,872 feet of elevation gain to
Slumgullion Pass; total of 17 miles and 3,380 feet of elevation
gain to Spring Creek Pass. At the Lake City Public Park one
block west, there are picnic tables, rest rooms, and nearby

museums and libraries in addition to standard tourist town fare. Lake City is home to a lot more history than just Alferd Packer and is remarkably franchise-free. The road leading west from the starting intersection is the Engineer Pass road, part of the Alpine Loop, a popular jeep road. The other leg of the loop is Weminuche County Road 30, 2.3 miles south on Colorado Highway 149.

South Side: Spring Creek Reservoir Picnic Ground (9,252 feet); 12.3 miles and 1,649 feet of elevation gain to Spring Creek Pass; total of 19 miles and 3,415 feet of elevation gain to Slumgullion Pass. Tiny picnic grounds sprout in the strangest places. This one is out in the middle of nowhere, but it is well positioned for riding both Spring Creek and Slumgullion Passes from the south (east). The grade begins to pick up here and both passes can be done without turning the day into a marathon. There is a large sign, tables, and rest rooms, but no water. The road and shoulder are excellent right here.

Alternate Start and Stop Points

North Side: Lake San Cristobal area (8,847 feet). Riding from here will provide 12.1 miles and 2,514 feet of elevation gain to Slumgullion pass; 18.7 miles and 3,191 feet of elevation gain to Spring Creek Pass. From the Lake City Public Park, go 2.3 miles south to a road that is the second of two that form the Alpine loop Jeep road. Turn right and go up this road for four miles. Here the pavement ends, and there is a large, well-shaded area on the right that has been camped on. This makes a good alternate start if you'd like to avoid Lake City. This area is right on the border of the National Forest, and there are no signs forbidding camping.

South Side: Silverthread Visitors Center (8,192 feet) at the junction of U.S. Highway 160 and Colorado Highway 149 in South Fork; 57.8 miles and 1,022 feet of elevation gain to Spring Creek Pass; total of 64.3 miles and 4,475 feet of elevation gain to Slumgullion Pass. This building, which looks like a small office complex, is set back from the highway by big lawns and even bigger parking lots. There are picnic tables outside beneath the flag, and water fountains and rest rooms indoors.

Palisade Campground and day-use area (8,360 feet) on Colorado Highway 149, 10.3 miles west of South Fork; 46.8 miles and 2,541 feet of elevation gain to Spring Creek Pass; total of 54 miles and 4,307 feet of elevation gain to Slumgullion Pass. These 10 miles just west of South Fork are no great loss; from here to Spring Creek Pass is the best of the upper Rio Grande valley. Spring Creek Pass is a way out, but most of it is flat.

Creede (8,841 feet) on Colorado Highway 149, 24 miles northwest of South Fork; 33.8 miles and 2,060 feet of elevation gain to Spring Creek Pass; total of 40.3 miles and 3,826 feet of elevation gain to Slumgullion Pass. Creede, a bit higher than the surrounding area, is a compact little town with everything you might need, except a bike store. There is a small park in the center of town; north of Creede is an underground mining museum and community center, which has what must be the world's sturdiest picnic tables.

Marshall Creek Campground (8,789 feet) on Colorado Highway 149, 6.3 miles southwest of Creede and 30.3 miles northwest of South Fork; 27.5 miles and 2,112 feet of elevation gain to Spring Creek Pass; total of 34 miles and 3,878 feet of elevation gain to Slumgullion Pass. This is the best camping outside Creede; it is a full-service, full-fee campground. Most of the land off the side of the highway is private, so it's best to take advantage of Forest Service campgrounds such as this when they show up.

Silverthread Campground and day-use area (9,879 feet) on South Clear Creek Road, off Colorado Highway 149, 2.6 miles west of Spring Creek Reservoir Picnic Area and 48.2 miles northwest of South Fork; 9.7 miles and 1,022 feet of elevation gain to Spring Creek Pass; total of 16.1 miles and 2,788 feet of elevation gain to Slumgullion Pass. This is the best place to camp if you want to ride both passes in the morning.

Road and Traffic Conditions

Spring Creek and Slumgullion Passes are unusual because they have both good roads and low traffic. Colorado Highway 149 is not a bustling commercial artery, and early in the morning, before the motor homes start rolling, you may get lucky and have the road to yourself. The steeper sections of Slumgullion are usually narrow, but because they also have extremely sharp curves, traffic is slow. The shoulders are generally small to nonexistent. The turns near the top can be dirty, but during the summer the road is very clean.

Descents

South Side: Neither side is exhilarating, but Spring Creek is beautiful. Most of the Rio Grande valley is more of a park than a valley.

North Side: Slumgullion, on the other hand, is steep and deceptive. The curves are signed conservatively instead of accurately. You can go through one set marked 20 miles per hour doing 40, and then get to another 20-miles-per-hour curve that really is a 20-miles-per-hour curve. Speed builds fast at 10 percent and 11 percent grades, but the sharp curves force a lot of braking. The road doesn't open up until lower down.

Sleep and Supplies

Things are kind of spread out around here, but there's plenty of tourist services and accommodations in Lake City, Creede (restaurants and shops), and South Fork. For more information on the north, call the Lake City–Hinsdale County Chamber, 970-944-2527. For the south contact Creede, 719-658-2874, or South Fork, 800-571-0882.

The north side is in the Gunnison National Forest, 970-874-6600, Gunnison Ranger District, 970-641-0474; the south side is in the Rio Grande National Forest, 719-852-5941, Divide Ranger District, 719-658-2556. There is dispersed camping from the Lake City area all the way to Spring Creek Pass. Slumgullion is a Forest Service dispersed campsite just off the pass of that name. Silverthread Campground is less than 10 miles south of Spring

Creek Pass. The Rio Grande valley is surprisingly treeless, so don't expect to pull off the road and settle in just anywhere. Marshal Creek and Rio Grande Reservoir Campgrounds are your best bet west of Creede.

MILEAGE LOG

★0   Intersection of Second and Gunnison in downtown Lake City (8,658 feet). One block west of here is the town central park, library, and bank. Plenty of parking, and everything you need (or don't need) is nearby. Go south on 149

0.5 Intersection of Main and Vine in Lake City is shockingly unfranchised.

1.3 Pullout.

☆2.3 Weminuche County Road 30 on the right to the Lake San Cristobal Recreation Area (8,847 feet), 4 miles up this road is a good alternate start/stop point).

2.6 Cross the Lake Fork of the Gunnison River and start going up.

2.8 Alferd Packer Massacre Site.

3.0 20 mph curve.

5.2 15 mph curve. Lake San Cristobal overlook.

6.0 Massive pullout and sign giving information on the area.

7.4 Leaving Gunnison National Forest.

8.3 Windy Point Forest Service overlook on the left.

9.3 The road is steep, narrow, and curved.

10.4 High point (11,530 feet). The whole summit of Slumgullion Pass is about 0.3 mile long.

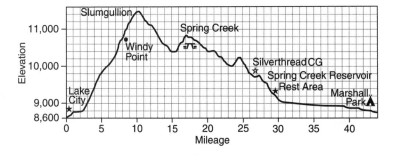

▲ 10.7 Slumgullion Pass (11,530 feet). Good dispersed camping around here. The road is good and the shoulder is narrow. The rest of the route is much more plateau-like than the steep curves of the north side.

12.2 Crest of a 25 mph curve. Mount Baldy Cinco is in the distance. There is often snow in this corridor of trees. Everything is deep, green, and cool—perfect summer riding.

14.0 Danny Carr Memorial Ski Trail. Nice mix of aspens and pines; good, easy curves.

14.8 Pullout and sign for Slumgullion Pass.

15.8 Oleo Ranch (fishing, hunting, horses, modern cabins).

▲ 17.2 Spring Creek Pass (10,901 feet). A useful picnic area here, especially since the Forest Service has either forgotten to post or has not yet posted "no camping" signs. Picnic tables, rest rooms, fire grates, enough trees for a little seclusion. The road shoulder and surface are excellent nearby and the traffic is sparse, especially in the morning.

17.8 Spring Creek Pass Corrals.

19.0 Pullout on the right.

22.3 Historical information; here it's a rolling, rambling, road.

23.5 Parking lot.

25.0 Scenic overlook.

☆ 26.8 South Clear Creek Road and Silverthread Campground and day-use area (9,879 feet) on the left. An excellent alternate start/stop point or camping spot.

★ 29.4 Spring Creek Reservoir Rest Site (9,252 feet) on the right. Look for the large sign and small pond. Picnic tables, toilets; no potable water.

33.0 Freemon's General Store, an isolated spot to find fishing tackle, burgers, laundry, ice cream, beer, sodas.

34.9 Very rough dirt road leads 5 miles to Rio Grande Reservoir Campground.

☆ 44.7 Middle Creek Road on the right. A short distance down this paved road is Marshall Creek Campground (8,789 feet). The best camping near Creede. Water should be available.

46.6 Cross the Rio Grande on a long bridge.

☆51.0 Creede (8,841 feet), a compact tourist town; a few restaurants, shops, a small central park with extra-sturdy picnic tables.

   61.3 Pullout near Cottonwood Cove (camping, cabins, rafts, charbroiled steaks, burgers, chicken).

   62.5 Blue Creek Lodge, restaurant, and cabins.

☆64.7 Palisade Campground and day-use area (8,360 feet). Water available.

☆75.0 Silverthread Visitors Center (8,192 feet) at the junction with U.S. Highway 160 in South Fork, which has anything you might need except a bike shop. U.S. 160 becomes more industrial as it heads east to Del Norte.

29 WOLF CREEK PASS
10,850 FEET

Wolf Creek Pass is monumental. Both sides are long, steep, and unrelenting. The mountain leans over this road, threatening to push it into the valley. Huge concrete barriers and a snowshed hold back or deflect the debris, but here anything man-made is puny. Cresting the top of Wolf Creek Pass is a happy relief and makes a day great. There are longer, higher, or steeper passes, but Wolf Creek is a nearly perfect combination.

NORTH TO SOUTH: Distance from Silverthread Visitors Center to Pagosa Springs: 42.8 miles

NORTH SIDE: Distance from Silverthread Visitors Center to Wolf Creek Pass: 19.4 miles

Elevation gain: 2,658 feet

Grades: Maximum 7.2%; average 3.2% for 2.6 miles, 4.4% for 2.2 miles, 6.4% for 3.6 miles

Difficulty: 3

SOUTH SIDE: Distance from Pagosa Springs to Wolf Creek Pass: 23.4 miles

Elevation gain: 3,737 feet

Grades: Maximum 7.8%; average 6.4% for 8.5 miles
Difficulty: 5

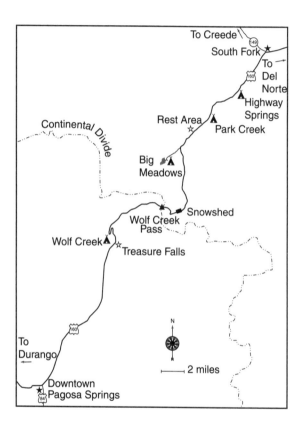

Recommended Start and Stop Points

North Side: Silverthread Visitors Center (8,192 feet) at the intersection of Colorado Highway 149 and U.S. Highway 160 in South Fork; 19.4 miles and 2,658 feet of elevation gain to Wolf Creek Pass. This building, which looks like a small office complex, is set back from the highway by big lawns and even bigger parking lots. There are picnic tables outside beneath the flag, and water fountains and rest rooms indoors.

South Side: Pagosa Springs Town Park (7,113 feet) along the north side of the San Juan River at the intersection of San Juan (Main) and Post Office Streets in Pagosa Springs; 23.4 miles and 3,737 feet of elevation gain to Wolf Creek Pass. The park has enough shade and river water to cool you down after a long ride. Look for a yellow gazebo. The rest of town is in easy walking distance.

Alternate Start and Stop Points

North Side: Rest area (8,579 feet) 9.7 miles southwest of South Fork, near orange gates used to close to the highway in winter; 9.7 miles and 2,271 feet of elevation gain to Wolf Creek Pass. Picnic tables. This alternate starting point cuts the distance exactly in half, but leaves more than the lion's share of the climbing.

South Side: Treasure Falls parking area (8,131 feet) on U.S. Highway 160, 15.3 miles northeast of Pagosa Springs between miles 159 and 158; 8.1 miles and 2,719 feet of elevation gain to Wolf Creek Pass. This is a busy place but people don't stay long, so even if the lot looks full, something will open up soon. From Pagosa Springs up to here, all the land off the road is private, so there aren't any other secluded spots in the woods just off the road. This area provides a good spot to get most of the elevation in and cut out all of the flat.

Road and Traffic Conditions

There is some of everything on this section of U.S. Highway 160. The worst section is low on the north side, 11 miles southwest of South Fork. The road has been paved but obviously has not been widened or straightened since it got a lot of horse-drawn wagon traffic. Unfortunately, now it's getting a lot of RV traffic, and it is somewhat tight through here. There are plenty of lanes and wide shoulders on the steep sections, however, so generally the higher you go, the easier it is for everybody to share the road. The surface is good overall, but despite this, U.S. 160 gets more than its share of rockfall and snowslides. Occasional scars and scrapes are big enough to get hold of a bike wheel. The snowshed just north (east) of the pass is a hazard because it is unlit. Like Monarch Pass (ride 23), Wolf Creek Pass gets precipitation early and often.

Descents

South Side: The top of Wolf Creek Pass is a launch pad. The southwest side has only two sharp curves to slow you down, and this is a good place for top speeds. There are enough lanes to use. Unfortunately, the traffic is also going fast and may want the same lane you want. Road hazards are more serious at 50 miles per hour with a truck breathing down your back.

North Side: Descending toward South Fork is fast off the top, but be ready for bad pavement at the snowshed after 2 miles. After 8 miles, the road narrows and clogs with traffic. This is frustrating because there is still a good grade and good curves.

Sleep and Supplies

South Fork on the north has everything you need except a bike shop. Pagosa Springs on the south is compact, and all the amenities are close to the recommended south-side start/stop point, a good place to get water. For more information on the area, call the South Fork Chamber of Commerce, 800-571-0881, or the Pagosa Springs Chamber of Commerce, 970-264-2360.

U.S. Highway 160 serves a huge area. The north side is in the Rio Grande National Forest, 719-852-5941, Divide Ranger District, 719-657-3321. The woods south (west) of the pass are run by the San Juan National Forest, 970-247-4874, Pagosa Ranger District, 970-264-2268. Roadside campgrounds are busy along this road. Highway Springs and Park Creek are close to U.S. 160 on the north side; Big Meadow is 2.5 miles from the highway on a dirt road. South of the pass, Wolf Creek Campground and Pagosa Campground are near the highway; East Fork Campground is off the highway.

MILEAGE LOG

★0   Silverthread Visitors Center (8,192 feet) at the junction

of U.S. Highway 160 and Colorado Highway 149 in South
Fork. Water, rest rooms, parking. Head south on U.S. 160.

0.7 Collection of restaurants and T-shirt shops.

1.4 Beaver Creek Road.

2.1 South Fork city limit.

4.0 Highway Springs Campground on the left.

4.3 Pullout.

5.1 Road is good but narrow through a tight canyon.

6.1 Cabin complex and massive RV megaplex. Full
hookups, laundry, TV, ice, horses, fishing, golf, riding, heavy
side road traffic.

7.4 Park Creek Road/Forest Service access road to
Summitville. Cross the bridge to a good alternate start.

7.8 Park Creek Campground on the left.

9.2 Gas station and groceries.

☆9.7 Pullout and rest area (8,579 feet) just before some
orange gates. This is right where the grade begins; a good
alternate start/stop point with picnic tables.

11.3 The road is good but the shoulder is minimal. This
major highway is little more than a paved country road
through here: quaint, but dangerous.

11.5 Big Meadow Reservoir Road on the right. Paved for
0.5 mile; Big Meadow Reservoir Campground is another
2 miles away on the dirt road. All other camping in this area
is prohibited.

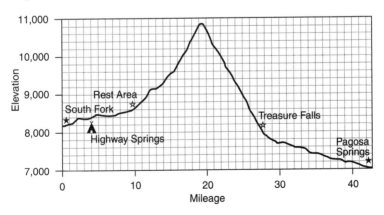

11.6 Large pullout.

13.4 Huge shoulder and pullout at the road to Tucker Ponds Campground and Recreation Area. From here on up is the steepest part of the grade.

17.0 Immense pullout. The road and shoulder are good.

17.3 Immense pullout.

17.5 Snowshed, basically an unlit tunnel that is long, dark, dripping wet, and sometimes icy; the road is always bad. This is dangerous on a north-side descent because your eyes do not adjust to the dark fast enough to see the rim-cracking potholes that are always there.

18.6 Wolf Creek Ski Area. Closed in summer, so, unlike many ski areas, there is no food, water, shopping, etc.

19.1 Scenic overlook at mile 167, with some good opportunities for dispersed camping.

▲ 19.4 Wolf Creek Pass (10,850 feet). This is a broad area, and most of what is flat is often marshy, even in autumn. Many pullout areas, a large sign detailing the efforts of people who had the misfortune of using mules instead of bikes to get up here. A good spot to get a drink, adjust your clothing and bike, and get ready for speed on the south-side descent.

21.4 Wolf Creek Road on the left. The grade is unrelenting and the shoulder is poor.

24.2 The road is generally in good shape, but there are a few surprises.

24.7 Massive barriers hold back debris.

24.9 Spectacular setting. Many pullouts through this area.

25.3 Beware big divots in the road, especially in the shadows.

25.4 Broken road surface.

25.7 25 mph curve with overlook and pullout.

☆27.5 Treasure Falls parking area (8,131 feet) on the left, and Windy Pass Road. Parking here is crowded.

32.2 Cross the West Fork of the San Juan River at the turnoff for East Fork Campground.

34.0 Turkey Creek Road on the right.

35.0 Pullout; excellent shoulder.

35.1 Jackson Mountain Road.

35.8 Middle of a picturesque valley.

38.4 Fawn Gulch Road.

40.6 Pagosa Campground.

41.9 Intersection with U.S. Highway 84, which leads south to Chromo.

42.4 San Juan National Forest information center. Rest rooms and water are available.

★42.8 Pagosa Springs Town Park (7,113 feet) at San Juan (Main) and Post Office Streets in Pagosa Springs. On the north side of the river. Look for the yellow gazebo. Rest rooms, shade, water from the river, a few riverside picnic tables.

30 LA MANGA and CUMBRES PASSES
10,230 feet and 10,022 feet

This route takes you about 10 miles into northern New Mexico at the ride's western end. The east side of these passes is a smooth river ride until you reach Horca; there the road shoots up as if suddenly remembering to gain elevation. The 7-mile-long area from La Manga Pass to Cumbres Pass is a carpet of wildflowers and an island of cool; you lose about 500 feet from La Manga, regaining about half of it to top out on Cumbres. There are no high, snowy peaks in sight, but these passes have the added interest of the nearby Cumbres Toltec Narrow Gauge Railroad. On the south side of La Manga, the road is near the railroad tracks all the way to Chama. Because the train runs frequently and keeps a good pace, it's not impossible to race alongside it.

NORTH TO SOUTH: Distance from Antonito Railroad Depot to U.S. Highway 84: 47.9 miles

NORTH SIDE: Distance from Antonito Railroad Depot to La Manga Pass: 27.4 miles; to Cumbres Pass, 34.5 miles

Elevation gain: To La Manga Pass, 2,275 feet; to Cumbres Pass, 2,067 feet net, 2,599 feet total

Grades: La Manga Pass, maximum 9%; average 2.8% for 1.3
    miles, 6.3% for 4.2 miles; Cumbres Pass, 3.2% (down) for
    3.2 miles, 3% (up) for 1.6 miles
Difficulty: 3
SOUTH SIDE: Distance from Chama Railroad Depot to
    Cumbres Pass: 11.9 miles; to La Manga Pass, 19 miles
Elevation gain: To Cumbres Pass, 2,154 feet; to La Manga Pass,
    2,362 feet net, 2,686 feet total
Grades: Cumbres Pass, maximum 6%; average 2.6% for 4.5
    miles, 4.4% for 4.8 miles, 4.8% for 1.5 miles; La Manga Pass,
    3% (down) for 1.6 miles, 3.2% (up) for 3.2 miles
Difficulty: 3

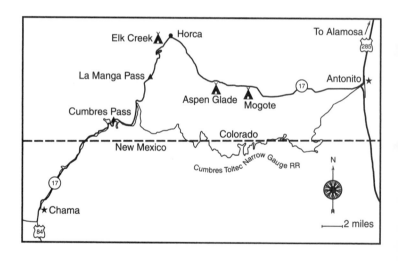

Recommended Start and Stop Points

North Side: Cumbres Toltec Narrow Gauge Railroad Depot
(7,955 feet) at the intersection of Colorado Highway 17 and U.S.
Highway 285 just south of San Antonito proper; 27.4 miles and
2,275 feet to La Manga Pass; total of 34.5 miles and 2,599 feet to
Cumbres Pass. There is a humongous parking area here for the
railroad; this day-use area has water towers, old trains, gift
shops, live llamas, and even pet sitting.

South Side: Cumbres Toltec Narrow Gauge Railroad Depot in the center of Chama (7,800 feet) on Colorado Highway 17; 11.9 miles and 2,154 feet of elevation gain to Cumbres Pass; total of 19 miles and 2,686 feet to La Manga Pass. This is the twin of the depot in Antonito—no llamas, though—and like Antonito, there is no overnight parking in the huge parking area for the railroad depot. Old-town Chama is dedicated to serving the railroad and the tourists it brings in. The main drag has gifts, restaurants, and nothing for bikes.

Alternate Start and Stop Points

North Side: Mogote Campground (8,436 feet) on Colorado Highway 17, 12.9 miles west of Antonito; 14.5 miles and 1,794 feet of elevation gain to La Manga Pass; total of 21.6 miles and 2,118 feet of elevation gain to Cumbres Pass. This national forest campground has all the usual facilities, including water. It is well positioned because it cuts out some of the flat but leaves some for a warm-up. This is not a day-use area, but there is a good pullout 0.3 mile before Mogote Campground.

Aspen Glade Campground (8,495 feet) on Colorado Highway 17, 15 miles west of Antonito; 12.4 miles and 1,735 feet of elevation gain to La Manga Pass; total of 19.5 miles and 2,059 feet of elevation gain to Cumbres Pass. This national forest campground has all the expected facilities, including water. It is also well positioned to cut out some of the flat but leave some for a warm-up. It is not a day-use area, but there is a good pullout 0.3 mile after Aspen Glade Campground.

Road and Traffic Conditions

Colorado Highway 17 is fairly quiet. There is agricultural traffic but few heavy trucks. The west side gets a lot of tourist traffic from people stopped to take pictures or videos of the train. Expect erratic driving and people wandering the highway with a camera stuck to one eye. Despite its small size, the road has a fair to good shoulder everywhere except some of the steepest sections north of La Manga Pass. There are rough spots, and track crossings become more frequent as you head south. The poor road is not so noticeable going up the La Manga side, but the road is badly cracked and has been patched with ribbons of tar. This makes a steady, jarring thu-thump that is like riding an old bike on a battered sidewalk.

Descents

South Side: From Cumbres Pass to Chama is a relaxing ride. It's not too steep or curved, but the hill country and long vistas of New Mexico open before you. You may see the train or just its manelike plume of smoke.

North Side: Riding down La Manga Pass to Antonito, however, is no place for reverie. There's one slowing curve, but for the most part it's a fast ride on poor pavement. A bridge at the bottom of the grade has a nasty, spoke-busting expansion joint.

Sleep and Supplies

Look for food and other services in Antonito, Horca (restaurant, grocery store, land office), and Chama (gifts, restaurants). For more information on the north (east) end, contact the Antonito Chamber of Commerce, 719-376-5475; in the south (west) end, contact Chama in New Mexico, 505-756-2306.

The route is in the Rio Grande National Forest, 719-852-5941, Conejos Peak Ranger District, 719-274-8971. Established campsites near the highway are Mogote, Aspen Glade, and Elk Creek, all on the north (east) side and all with the usual facilities, including water. Dispersed camping is possible between the two summits, but the sheep have probably gotten there first. There's no public camping areas south (west) of Cumbres Pass, but there's a private RV campground near Chama.

MILEAGE LOG

★0   Cumbres Toltec Narrow Gauge Railroad Depot (7,955 feet) just south of Antonito and east of the junction of Colorado Highway 17 and U.S. Highway 285. A vast parking lot, but no overnight parking. Head west on Highway 17.

4.1 Mogote, a town of only a few cabins.

4.6 Cross the Conejos River.

5.9 The road surface is okay and the shoulder is small.

7.5 Sage and butte country, fairly flat.

10.2 Excellent shoulder by the river. It is shady and there's nothing man-made.

12.1 Fox Creek Store in Fox Creek, a newly created town.

12.6 Good pullout as you enter Rio Grande National Forest.

☆12.9 Mogote Campground (8,436 feet) on the left. Fully equipped; picnic tables, water.

☆15.0 Aspen Glade Campground (8,495 feet) on the left. Also fully equipped; picnic tables, water.

15.3 Pullout on the right.

17.8 Gentle curves through woodland and along the river.

20.9 Generous pullout on the left.

21.4 Town of Horca (restaurant, grocery, land office) at the intersection with the road to Platoro. No public park or areas.

21.9 Cross the bridge over the Conejos River. The road goes up dramatically, or at least it looks impressive because the road has been so flat up to now. This bridge has deep, sharp expansion gaps. The road is cracked and broken and the shoulder is small.

22.6 Pulloff on the right. Good views as soon as you begin climbing.

24.4 Pullout and scenic overlook. The road is rougher near the top and constrained by guardrails, jersey barriers, and gravel.

26.2 Road flattens out. Begin the summit plateau.

27.0 Road on the right.

▲27.4 La Manga Pass (10,230 feet), a large flat area. If you want to camp, you'll have to find an area that isn't heavily used by livestock. There are also many flowers along the road in early summer.

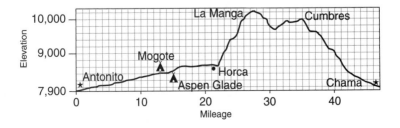

28.0 Red Lake Trail Road. Wet, marshy area with wildflowers and spruce trees.

30.4 Low point between the two passes (9,700 feet). There is a prominent curve at the Cumbres Resort development, and the railroad tracks come into view.

34.3 Trujillo Meadows Reservoir.

▲ 34.5 Cumbres Pass (10,022 feet). A small train service area here and a place for passengers to get on and off. Rather than high peaks in the distance, the rolling hills of New Mexico are ahead.

38.9 Pullout.

40.0 Entering New Mexico.

40.2 Cross railroad tracks. The road is rough here, but the shoulder is wide. The road improves ahead.

41.3 Road to the right, giving access to the railroad tracks. While the train is running, expect many camera-equipped tourists stopped along the road taking pictures.

44.3 Emerge from the confines of the canyon and into the sagebrush country of New Mexico.

45.6 Cross railroad tracks.

45.8 Chama city limit.

46.1 Rio Chama RV Park.

★ 46.4 Cumbres Toltec Narrow Gauge Railroad Depot (7,868 feet) in the center of downtown Chama.

47.9 Intersection with Colorado Highway 64/U.S. Highway 84, which leads west and north to Chromo and Pagosa Springs.

31 COAL BANK and MOLAS PASSES
10,630 feet and 10,910 feet

Riding these two passes without stopping is hard to do. The grades are stout and long, and the sight of the San Juans will stop anyone in their tracks. Seen from the top of Coal Bank

Pass, Twilight Peak is especially impressive. As this road climbs, valleys fall away precipitously, air thins, and mountains loom and turn one behind the other. These passes are commonly ridden together—often as part of the San Juan Skyway loop; as described in this book, it's the first leg of the loop (so it's ridden south to north rather than the other way around)—but you can break them up by camping near Molas Pass. It is almost a shame that you can ride these two in one day. It would be better to spend a few weeks up here. The Andrews Lake area is a great place for lunch. For the other legs of the San Juan Skyway, see Red Mountain Pass (ride 32), Dallas Divide (ride 33), and Lizard Head Pass (ride 34).

SOUTH TO NORTH: Distance from Gateway Park and Visitors Center to Silverton: 49.4 miles

SOUTH SIDE: Distance from Gateway Park and Visitors Center to Coal Bank Pass: 35.6 miles; to Molas Pass, 42.9 miles

Elevation gain: To Coal Bank Pass, 4,167 feet; to Molas Pass, 4,454 feet net, 5,577 feet total

Grades: Coal Bank Pass, maximum 7.8%; average 3.7% for 7.3 miles, 6.5% for 5.5 miles, 7.8% for 1.3 miles; Molas Pass, 5.5% (down) for 2.9 miles, 5.3% (up) for 4 miles

Difficulty: 5

NORTH SIDE: Distance from Silverton to Molas Pass: 6.5 miles; to Coal Bank Pass, 13.8 miles

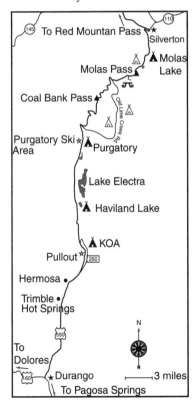

Elevation gain: To Molas Pass, 1,682 feet; to Coal Bank Pass,
    1,395 feet net, 2,265 feet total
Grades: Molas Pass, maximum 8%; average 2.1% for 1.7 miles,
    5.9% for 1 mile, 6% for 3.7 miles; Coal Bank Pass, 5.3%
    (down) for 4 miles, 5.5% (up) for 2.9 miles
Difficulty: 2

Recommended Start and Stop Points

South Side: Gateway Park and Visitors Center (6,463 feet)
on U.S. Highway 160, 0.7 mile east of Durango; 35.6 miles and
4,167 feet of elevation gain to Coal Bank Pass; total of 42.9 miles
and 5,577 feet of elevation gain to Molas Pass. There are many
places to get started in Durango: stores, malls, parks, side
streets, anywhere. Gateway Park is a huge area close to the
Animas River that always has some parking, plus water, picnic
tables, rest rooms, and tons of local information. The disadvantage is having to ride all the way through town with its myriad
stoplights and heavy traffic. From the intersection of U.S.
Highways 160 and 550, head north on U.S. 550 and turn right
on Twelfth to find a small but pleasant park at Twelfth and
Main. You can continue north and turn left on Nineteenth to
reach another park.

North Side: Silverton Visitors Center (9,228 feet) at the
intersection of U.S. Highway 550 and Colorado Highway 110 in
Silverton; 6.5 miles and 1,682 feet of elevation gain to Molas
Pass; total of 13.8 miles and 2,265 feet of elevation gain to Coal
Bank Pass. This is the easiest place to find and park in Silverton.
There is plenty of parking, rest rooms, and some interesting old
photos inside. Silverton gets busy when the mighty Durango to
Silverton Narrow-Gauge Railroad train comes to town.

Alternate Start and Stop Points

South Side: Small pullout (7,124 feet) on the left (west) side of
U.S. Highway 550, 15.6 miles north of Durango; 19.3 miles and
3,506 feet of elevation gain to Coal Bank Pass; total of 26.6 miles
and 4,916 feet of elevation gain to Molas Pass. This is between
the two intersections of County Road 250 on the right. There is

Twilight Peak near Coal Bank Pass.

nothing attractive about this spot except that it cuts out the flats just outside of Durango and gets you climbing immediately.

Purgatory Ski Area (8,744 feet) on the left side of U.S. Highway 550, 27 miles north of Durango; 7.8 miles and 1,897 feet of elevation gain to Coal Bank Pass; total of 15.1 miles and 3,307 feet of elevation gain to Molas Pass. This is an excellent mid-point. It is always cooler than the valley below, and there are enough shops, facilities, and parking to make things easy.

Road and Traffic Conditions

There's plenty of room on U.S. Highway 550 for everyone, but the road from Molas to Silverton is narrow in places. The surface can be rough on the ascent from Durango and into Silverton. Between Molas Pass and Silverton, the road is cut into very steep walls, and rocks on the road are common. Much of the traffic on U.S. 550 is recreational, so early in the morning it is generally light in the mountains. Traffic is heaviest between Durango and Purgatory because there are so many residences along the highway. There is a pullout on the top of Coal Bank Pass where nearly everyone stops. This area is a zoo, especially because visibility is limited when pulling on or off the highway.

Descents

North Side: From Molas to Silverton, the road isn't curved or switchbacked, but it does constantly weave back and forth trying to stick close to the canyon wall. This puts you in traffic on a narrow road.

South Side: From Coal Bank to Durango are the best turns of the two passes and, combined with the grade, they will test the tires. The break in the grade at Purgatory is almost a relief, but the last drop into the Animas valley is straight, straight speed.

Sleep and Supplies

Along U.S. Highway 550 itself the area is well equipped, but there are no facilities between the two passes. You'll find food and supplies at Durango, Hermosa (market, gas station), and Silverton (a full-service tourist town). For more information, call Durango Area Chamber of Commerce, 970-247-0312, in the south; for Silverton in the north, call 970-387-5654.

U.S. Highway 550 is within the San Juan National Forest, 970-247-4874, Columbine Ranger District, 970-247-4874. Forest

Service campgrounds are busy through here. Haviland Lake, Purgatory, and Molas Lake Campgrounds all have the usual facilities. There is some dispersed camping along Old Lime Creek Road (at mileage points 30.2 and 38.5 in the mileage log), but the road is rough dirt, and sites near the highway will likely be taken.

MILEAGE LOG

★0   Gateway Park and Visitors Center (6,463 feet), on U.S. Highway 160 east of Durango. Water, tables, rest rooms, tons of local information. No camping or overnight parking.

☆0.7 Junction with U.S. Highway 550 in Durango. A large City Market, other stores, hotels; confusing, twisted roads. Head north on U.S. 550.

1.1 Ninth Street and Mall World.

1.8 Intersection with Twelfth.

2.2 Intersection with Main Street. A good park is near here.

2.5 Pleasant town park on the left. No water but plenty of shade. Parking may be tight later in the day or on weekends.

3.1 Twenty-fifth Street. Going west, this road becomes La Plata County Road 204, a pleasant residential road, but it's paved for only 3.5 miles. The nearest Forest Service campground is another mile up this steep dirt road. Dispersed camping is allowed another 4 miles after that.

3.8 The road to Fort Lewis College.

4.7 Camping opportunities for the stealthy and observant.

5.4 Leaving Durango.

9.9 Trimble Hot Springs on the left.

11.5 Small settlement of Hermosa (market, gas station) on the left.

11.9 Cross narrow-gauge railroad tracks.

12.9 Leaving the hot Plains behind.

15.1 Intersection with County Road 250 on the right, which leads to KOA camping before looping back to the highway.

☆16.3 Small pullout (7,124 feet) on the left; this alternate start/stop point eliminates the flats outside of Durango.

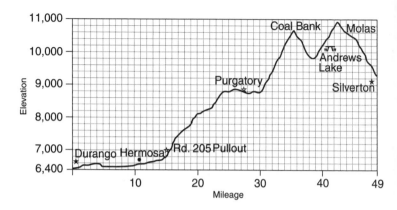

16.9 Intersection with the other end of County Road 250 on the right.

25.2 Convenience store bustling with jeeps, motorcycles, dogs, and kids. This is a good place to water up.

☆27.8 Purgatory Ski Area (8,744 feet). A small mall, a few restaurants operate all year long. Coffee, easy parking. Things also get steep soon.

28.4 Hermosa Park Road; National Forest access. Camping is several miles up this dirt road.

29.6 Cascade Grill and Cascade Village.

30.1 Cascade Creek Road; National Forest access.

30.2 Old Lime Creek Road; National Forest access. Rough road for bikes but good dispersed camping through here.

32.8 The world becomes cooler and alpine.

▲35.6 Coal Bank Pass (10,630 feet). A road near the pass leads to dispersed camping. A little area up here to park and look around. Twilight Peak is spectacular through the trees.

36.1 Sign for Twilight Peak.

37.4 The road is rough and the shoulder is intermittent.

38.4 Low point (9,787 feet) between Coal Bank and Molas Passes.

38.5 Old Lime Creek Road; National Forest access.

39.6 Major turn (10,000 feet).

40.4 Two lanes up, one down. The road is fair.

41.3 Rest area among the aspens. The road is grubby through here.

41.8 Pullout.

42.0 Road to Andrews Lake and Picnic Area on the right. This one-lane paved road leads shortly to Andrews Lake Scenic area; an idyllic little lake with paved walkways, picnic tables, rest rooms, informative plaques. This is a well-developed area.

▲ 42.9 Molas Pass (10,910 feet). A small viewing area and, unsurprisingly, good views.

43.3 Road for Little Molas Lake on the left. A short dirt road leads to excellent dispersed camping and a small lake along the Colorado Trail.

44.0 Molas Lake Trail.

44.5 Molas Lake Campground, a private campground and lake with stunning views. A small country store; fishing at the lake.

45.5 See the San Juans. Stop here.

45.7 Pullout.

47.3 The road is pretty, but rough. Good curves.

49.1 Large pullout.

★ 49.4 Silverton Visitors Center (9,228 feet), directly across the street from the intersection of U.S. Highways 110 and 550.

32 RED MOUNTAIN PASS
11,081 FEET

Red Mountain Pass is the jewel of the San Juan Skyway; as the loop is presented in this book, Red Mountain is the second leg, described from south to north. From Silverton to the summit is merely a pristine roadway cut through some of the most spectacular mountains in the state. The north side is merely the most spectacular, fun, hilariously twisted, and breathtaking road that two bike tires will ever touch. Between the pass and Ironton Flats, the road is so tightly curved that it looks as though it follows an old Indian trail, but the lower portion plunges straight down a glacial gash streaming with waterfalls. There are many mines along the road, which add some historical flavor too. For the other legs of the San Juan Skyway, see Coal Bank and Molas Passes (ride 31), Dallas Divide (ride 33), and Lizard Head Pass (ride 34).

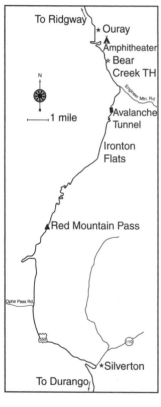

SOUTH TO NORTH: Distance from Silverton to Ridgway: 33.7 miles

SOUTH SIDE: Distance from Silverton to Red Mountain Pass: 10 miles

Elevation gain: 1,877 feet

Grades: Maximum 6.7%; average 2.2% for 2.6 miles, 2.3% for 3.5 miles, 5.6% for 2.3 miles, 6.5% for 1.4 miles

Difficulty: 2

NORTH SIDE: Distance from Ridgway to Red Mountain Pass: 23.7 miles

Elevation gain: 4,097 feet

Grades: Maximum 8.4%; average 2% for 5.2 miles, 5.9% for 4.5 miles, 6% for 6 miles

Difficulty: 5

Recommended Start and Stop Points

South Side: Silverton Visitors Center (9,228 feet) at the intersection of U.S. Highway 550 and Colorado Highway 110 in Silverton; 10 miles and 1,877 feet of elevation gain to Red Mountain Pass. This is the easiest place to find and park in Silverton, the destination for the Durango to Silverton Narrow-Gauge Railroad—when the train comes in, the town is busy. There's water, rest rooms, plenty of parking, and a lot of interesting old pictures inside.

North Side: Mountain Market (6,961 feet) across from the city park in central Ridgway, 0.4 mile west of U.S. Highway 550 and Colorado Highway 62; 23.7 miles and 4,097 feet of elevation gain to Red Mountain Pass. Starting from Ridgway adds some flat mileage, but a warm-up is a good idea on this ride, and Ridgway is no slouch when it comes to good views. The San Juan Bakery and Café is next to the market. The city park has everything you might need except overnight parking. You can park overnight in the market parking lot if you take the spaces farthest from the store.

Alternate Start and Stop Points

North Side: Ouray Visitors Information Center (7,754 feet) on the north side of town on the right side of U.S. Highway 550; 13.5 miles and 3,327 feet of elevation gain to Red Mountain Pass. Ouray is the place to start if you can't wait to get into the mountains. The road through town is steep. The visitors' information center shares a parking lot with a park and the Ouray Hot Springs and Fitness Pool.

Bear Creek Trailhead (8,414 feet) on the right side of U.S. 550, 3 miles south of the Ouray Visitors Information Center, near mile 91; 11.8 miles and 2,667 feet of elevation gain to Red Mountain Pass. If you'd like to start on the southern outskirts of Ouray, there is parking at this trailhead.

Road and Traffic Conditions

This portion of U.S. Highway 550 is in good shape, but it is narrow—and sometimes narrower than narrow. The section north of Ironton Flats is carved into solid granite. Big trucks cannot help but take some of the oncoming lane, and in many places the curves are blind. There are sparse, hanging pull-outs along the way, so as you go up, you may have to pull over to let cars pass. There are few guardrails and the drop-offs are big, so don't pull over too far. Unfortunately, U.S. 550 is a fairly busy road. Besides truck and motor-home traffic, people can be out taking pictures at scenic pullouts or in odd, unexpected places.

Descents

North Side: You'll be going faster than the cars. This road is steep and features the tightest 10-miles-per-hour curves this side of Mount Evans. Be prepared to slow suddenly as you get to the end of Ironton Flats; there is a series of traffic-stopping curves here. The lower grade is only a little longer and a little steeper than the upper portion, but it is much more intense because it is closed in by the canyon wall on the right and empty space on the left. The lower portion is like careening down a waterslide. It is impossible not to use the entire lane, so be prepared to deal with cars in front and behind you.

South Side: The south side is not nearly as intense. There is only one sharp curve and the good grade will keep you moving.

Sleep and Supplies

Look for food, services, and supplies in Silverton (a full-service tourist town), Ouray, and Ridgway. For more information on the

Cyclists' heaven—Red Mountain Pass.

south side, call the Silverton Chamber of Commerce, 870-387-5654. To the north contact Ouray Chamber of Commerce, 970-325-4746, or Ridgway Chamber of Commerce, 970-626-3681.

This area is in the Uncompahgre National Forest, 970-874-6600, Ouray Ranger District, 970-240-5300. There's not much camping along this road because there aren't any level spots. There is one Forest Service site, Amphitheater, on the right between Bear Creek Trailhead and the Ouray Visitors Information Center; this has good camping and is a good spot to start from the north side. Kimber Ridge Campground in Ouray is a private, RV-oriented campground. There is also camping at Ridgway Reservoir State Park, 970-626-5822, north of Ridgway on U.S. Highway 550; this is a big area for big vehicles.

MILEAGE LOG

★0   Silverton Visitors Center (9,228 feet) at the intersection of Colorado Highway 110 and U.S. Highway 550. Plenty of parking, water. Head north on U.S. 550.

0.2 Silverton city limits.

0.4 Small road to the left leads to Mineral Creek.

1.1 The Columbine, a ghost restaurant.

2.0 San Juan County Road 7 on the left, with Forest Service access to South Mineral Creek.

3.1 Small road to the right.

4.9 Ophir Pass Road, Forest Service access.

6.7 Flat grade.

6.9 Old buildings. The road is poor and gets narrower.

7.6 Prominent 20 mph curve.

9.0 Road is extremely narrow.

9.1 House on the right.

9.7 Start climbing.

9.8 Black Bear Pass 4x4 road.

▲10.0 Red Mountain Pass (11,081 feet). Room to park and an old mine shaft to inspect, as well as a few signs giving the history of the pass. Good views and a good road ahead.

10.8 Junk on the road; rough road.

11.8 Iditarod Mine.

12.4 Rough road and not much shoulder.

13.0 10 mph curve and many more such ahead.

13.9 Pullout. This is a beautiful spot.

14.0 10,000 feet.

16.3 Ironton Flats; meadow, straight and flat.

16.6 Cross well-named Red Mountain Creek.

16.8 Pullout.

17.5 Pullout and Memorial for snowplow drivers.

17.6 Avalanche tunnel; beware road debris.

17.9 Tunnel ends; snow in summer.

18.4 The canyon is extremely tight; 20 mph curves, steep rock walls, and waterfalls are all around.

18.9 Old sluice box.

19.2 Engineer Mountain road on the right. This is part of the Alpine loop, a popular 4x4 route.

19.6 The road is carved into the canyon wall. Very tight.

20.2 Pullout and viewing area. Beware slow cars and gawking people.

☆20.6 Bear Creek Trailhead (8,414 feet), just before a tunnel. Parking here at this alternate start/stop point.

21.2 15 mph curve. Spectacular, fun, the best.

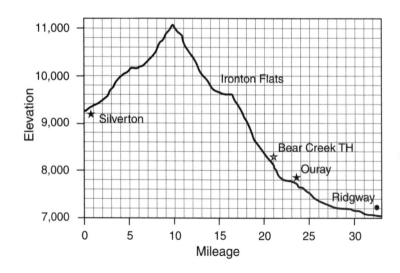

21.7 Historic Lookout Point. The road is so narrow that rocks and bushes stick out over it.

21.8 Amphitheater Campground on the right. Good camping; a good spot to start/stop.

22.5 Road 361 to Yankee Boy Basin and Camp Bird mine.

22.7 The grade ends.

22.8 Entering Ouray.

23.2 Main and Seventh.

☆23.5 Ouray Visitors Information Center (7,754 feet), which shares a parking lot with Ouray Hot Springs and Fitness Pool and a public park. This is the best place to park if you want to start from Ouray; no overnight parking, however.

24.0 Kimber Ridge Campground (private; RV-oriented) on the right.

24.8 Ouray Rotary Park. Picnic tables, no overnight parking.

27.7 Intersection with Ouray County Road 23.

31.8 Orvis Hot Springs. This stretch of road is hot in the summer, but there is always a good view of the Sneffels Range near Ridgway.

33.3 Intersection with Colorado Highway 62 on the left. Traffic is fast and constant; there's construction traffic in the morning and tourist traffic in the afternoon. Turn left on Highway 62.

★33.7 Mountain Market (6,961 feet) in Central Ridgway, next to the San Juan Bakery and Cafe; a park is across the way.

33 DALLAS DIVIDE
8,970 FEET

Riding passes usually means going through a mountain range. Dallas Divide, although a good hill, doesn't go up and over a range, it goes along the crest of one. Riding Colorado Highway 62 is a good way to see the spectacular Sneffels Range from every angle. Dallas Divide is a good warm-up to the more substantial passes of the San Juan Skyway, and is best ridden not on its own but as part of that loop; it's the third leg of the loop as it's described in this book. For the other legs, see Coal Bank and Molas Passes (ride 31), Red Mountain Pass (ride 32), and Lizard Head Pass (ride 34).

EAST TO WEST: Distance from Ridgway to Placerville: 23.1 miles

EAST SIDE: Distance from Ridgway to Dallas Divide: 10.3 miles

Elevation gain: 2,009 feet

Grades: Maximum 7.3%; average 3.5% for 2 miles, 6.4% for 3.4 miles

Difficulty: 2

WEST SIDE: Distance from Placerville to Dallas Divide: 12.8 miles

Elevation gain: 1,709 feet

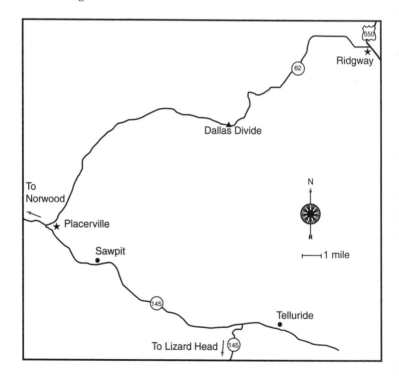

Grades: Maximum 5.5%; average 2.3% for 5.3 miles, 3.0% for
    6.6 miles
Difficulty: 1

Recommended Start and Stop Points

East Side: Mountain Market across from the city park in central Ridgway (6,961 feet), 0.4 mile west of U.S. Highway 550 and Colorado Highway 62; 10.3 miles and 2,009 feet of elevation gain to Dallas Divide. The city park has everything you might need except overnight parking. You can park overnight in the market parking lot if you take the spaces farthest from the store. The San Juan Bakery and Café is next to the market.

West Side: Intersection of Colorado Highways 62 and 145 in Placerville (7,261 feet); 12.8 miles and 1,709 feet of elevation gain to Dallas Divide. Placerville doesn't offer much of anything for the cyclist, and this point is included mostly as a convenient endpoint for elevation and distance information. The road from Placerville to Telluride is unpleasantly poor. A few miles before Telluride, Highway 145 splits. Continue east to Telluride or turn south to start up Lizard Head Pass. The east/south split of Highway 145 is 12.8 miles east of Placerville.

Alternate Start and Stop Points

None. Highway 145 from Placerville east into Telluride is unpleasantly poor.

Road and Traffic Conditions

Colorado Highway 62 is spacious and not too busy, a good road to cruise and watch the mountains go by. There are many scenic overlooks from which to make good photos. The area has little tree cover and can be windy. This is a poor place to get caught in the rain because all the surrounding land is private and there is no place to take shelter. Colorado Highway 145 from Sawpit to Telluride is so narrow that the white line is nearly falling off the side of the mountain, and thanks to a steady stream of heavy truck traffic, this stretch of road is probably the most unnerving in the state.

Descents

West Side: Because of the light grade into Placerville, it's possible to keep some speed, but generally this road was made for moseying.

East Side: Except for a short section, the road is straight and not too steep.

Sleep and Supplies

Food and supplies can be had in Ridgway, but Placerville doesn't offer much of anything for the cyclist. There is little, if any, opportunity for shelter until Telluride, southeast of Placerville. For more information, call the Ridgway Area Chamber of Commerce, 970-626-3681.

The only camping is at Ridgway Reservoir State Park, 970-626-5822, a couple miles north of Ridgway on U.S. Highway 550. This is a big area for big vehicles.

MILEAGE LOG

★0   Mountain Market in central Ridgway (6,961 feet), 0.4 mile west of U.S. Highway 550 and Colorado Highway 62. Ride west on Highway 62.

0.7 Ridgway city limit.

4.4 Dallas Creek Road on the left; National Forest access.

5.8 West Dallas Creek; National Forest access.

7.0 Intersection with County Road 24.

9.3 Huge pullout and a good place to view the Sneffels Range.

10.1 Scenic overlook. Both the pavement and the shoulder are good here.

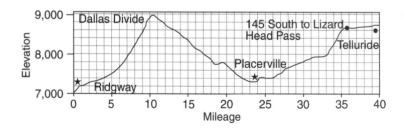

▲ 10.3 Dallas Divide (8,970 feet).

11.7 Last Dollar Road on the left; National Forest access.

14.9 Huge pullout and cattle chutes.

23.1 Intersection with Colorado Highway 145 in Placerville (7,261 feet).

35.7 East/south split of Highway 145.

39.7 Telluride Town Park in Telluride.

34 LIZARD HEAD PASS
10,250 FEET

The north side of Lizard Head Pass is dominated by Telluride and everything that surrounds a major ski town: traffic, construction, and land restrictions. All this makes the north side of Lizard Head the most unpleasant stretch of road on the San Juan Skyway. Hopefully this will improve, but roads rarely keep up with development. This is not an especially damning criticism, however, because the San Juan Skyway is beautiful enough to redeem anything. As the loop is described in this book, Lizard Head Pass is the fourth leg; for the other legs see Coal Bank and Molas Passes (ride 31), Red Mountain Pass (ride 32), and Dallas Divide (ride 33). The southern half of Lizard Head Pass is great for big-ring cruising along a road that can feel positively lonely. There are some gorgeous lakes and views along the way, which are often obscured by rain. To close the loop of the San Juan Skyway, you ride east from Dolores to Durango; however, this last leg isn't covered in this book because it doesn't go over a high point or pass (Target Tree is midway between Dolores and Durango).

NORTH TO SOUTH: Distance from Telluride Town Park to
    Flanders Park in Dolores: 65.6 miles
NORTH SIDE: Distance from Telluride to Lizard Head Pass:
    16 miles
Elevation gain: 1,592 feet

Grades: Maximum 5.6%; average 3.6% for 2.1 miles, 4.6% for
   1.3 miles, 5.4% for 3 miles, 5.6% for 2.4 miles
Difficulty: 2
SOUTH SIDE: Distance from Flanders Park in Dolores to
   Lizard Head Pass: 49.2 miles
Elevation gain: 3,270 feet
Grades: Maximum 7%; average 1% for 42.5 miles, 2.3% for 3.3
   miles, 7% for 1 mile
Difficulty: 4

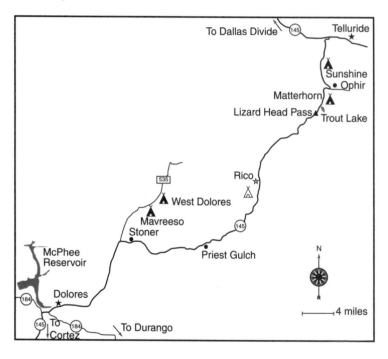

Recommended Start and Stop Points

North Side: Telluride Town Park and Nordic ski area (8,658
feet) on Colorado Highway 145, 3.8 miles east of the intersection
with Colorado Highway 62; 16 miles and 1,592 feet of elevation
gain to Lizard Head Pass. You'll go through most of Telluride to
get here, but there is a bike path alongside the highway.

South Side: Flanders Park and Dolores Visitors Information Center (6,980 feet) at Fifth and Railroad/Colorado Highway 145 in Dolores's city center; 49.2 miles and 3,270 feet of elevation gain to Lizard Head Pass. It's hard to miss because of the Galloping Goose, a train/car parked out front. The library is in front of the town park, which is close to restaurants and a grocery store. There is even a German bakery and a laundry. The town is big enough to have everything and small enough to find it easily. The weather gets hot here.

Alternate Start and Stop Points

North Side: Sunshine Campground (9,544 feet) on Colorado Highway 145 about 5 miles east and south of Colorado Highways 62 and 145; 7.3 miles and 706 feet of elevation gain to Lizard Head Pass. This full-service Forest Service campground is a good spot because it is right between Telluride and the pass. It's on top of the hump between Telluride and Ophir. The net gain to the tantalizingly close pass is 706 feet, but you'll lose and regain another 300 feet.

South Side: Marveeso Campground (7,640 feet) 6.2 miles northwest of Colorado Highway 145 on the West Dolores River Valley Road, which is 12.5 miles northeast of Dolores between miles 24 and 23 at a bridge where the West Dolores River meets the Dolores River; 42.5 miles and 2,610 feet of elevation gain to Lizard Head Pass. The newly paved road northwest up the West Dolores River valley is absolutely magnificent; it's too bad it's only paved for 13 miles, but it leads to excellent campgrounds that are well worth the curvaceous detour. San Juan West Dolores Campground is another 1.2 miles up the road. Both campgrounds are spacious, and there is plenty of opportunity for dispersed camping nearby. The weather gets hot farther south.

Rico (8,779 feet) on Colorado Highway 145, 36.3 miles northeast of Dolores; 12.5 miles and 1,471 feet of elevation gain to Lizard Head Pass. The Dolores River valley is long, and Rico is a good place to resupply. There is dispersed camping south of town and a Forest Service Information Center just north of town. Everyone here seems to have either a dog or a beard.

Road and Traffic Conditions

Colorado Highway 145 is a road that shows its wear. The north side has gotten some fresh pavement, but it won't stay fresh for long. It's a small narrow road subject to heavy traffic and heavier snows. The traffic gets lighter as Telluride gets farther away, but the road always has a rough, spot-maintenance feel to it. Things open up and get lonely south of Rico.

Descents

South Side: There's a short, steep section, and that's it. The rest is cruising on grades of 1 to 2 percent. Wind and weather have a much bigger impact on speed than the road itself.

North Side: The descent is sporting. There's a lot of up and down, side to side, and traffic, as well as a gritty road. The steep sections are so short that you'll never really be blazing down this road but always maneuvering and sometimes climbing.

Sleep and Supplies

Food and services can be found in Ridgway (market, cafe), Telluride, Ophir, Rico (theater, hotels, beer, land office), Stoner (lodge, bar, cafe, RV park), and Dolores (restaurants, bakery, grocery store, Laundromat). For more information on the north side, call the Ridgway Area Chamber of Commerce, 970-626-3681. For the Dolores area, contact the Dolores River Valley Chamber of Commerce, 970-882-4018.

The north side of this road is in the Uncompahgre National Forest, 970-874-6600, Norwood Ranger District, 970-327-4261. There are two accessible campgrounds, Sunshine and Matterhorn. The south side is part of San Juan National Forest, 970-247-4874, Dolores/Mancos Ranger District, 970-882-7296. There is some dispersed camping, but the best campsites are up the West Dolores River, at Marveeso Campground and San Juan West Dolores Campground. There is little camping between Stoner and Dolores.

MILEAGE LOG

★0   Telluride Town Park (8,658 feet) on Colorado Highway 145. Ride west on the bike path adjacent to the highway. The road out of Telluride, like most of the roads surrounding it, is bad.

☆3.8 East/south split of 145. There is a pullout/parking area here, but this intersection is busy. Head south on Highway 145.

4.7   25-mph curve; steep. The pavement is better here because it has been newly repaved.

5.6   Mountain Village. Gondola, skier parking. This looks like a fortress.

☆8.7 Sunshine Campground (9,544 feet).

9.7   Series of 25 mph curves. Bad road.

10.6 Forest Service road for Illium and Ames.

12.1 The road is steep and cuts deeply into a rock wall. Expect debris.

12.9 Matterhorn Campground on the right.

14.1 Turnoff for the Trout Lake area on the right. This is a beautiful area, privately run.

15.1 The road surface is little better than dirt.

▲16.0 Lizard Head Pass (10,250 feet). Parking area, signs describing the San Juan Skyway. An access road leads off to the left. There are supposed to be good views from here, but every time I've been here it's been raining hard.

18.1 East Fork Trailhead.

19.0 Pullout on left. The road steepens.

19.3 The road improves.

20.5 Pullout on left.

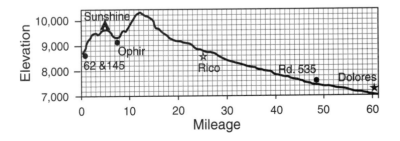

21.5 Intersection of Forest Service road to Dunton, 10 miles away.

21.8 Forest Service road to Barlow Creek Canyon Campground. There is a spot to park here.

22.8 Crossing Coal Creek.

26.9 Forest Service Information Center for San Juan National Forest.

☆28.5 Entering the town of Rico (8,779 feet). Theater, hotels, beer, land office.

29.3 Rico Cemetery and city limit. A picnic table is visible from the road south of the cemetery. This appears to be a public area and there is excellent, and so far hassle free, dispersed camping along the river.

31.3 Forest Service road to Scotch Creek on the left. There is a spot to pull off and park for the trailhead.

34.1 Crossing the Dolores River. Shoulder improves but the road is still lousy.

35.4 Green Snowasis, a store with books, crafts, snacks. It may or may not be open.

37.3 Large pullout at Road 435, Forest Service road to Roaring Fork.

38.6 Hillside Drive, Forest Service access road.

40.3 Crossing Priest Creek. Priest Creek Gulch and Campgrounds, a private enterprise, has a camp store.

41.9 Bear Creek Trailhead. There is a bridge across the river and a place to park.

43.0 Large pullout overlooking the river.

43.5 The grade decreases.

45.3 The shoulder is large but cracked and crummy.

46.2 Intersection with Forest Service Road 545, Taylor Creek Road.

50.1 Stoner, home of Stoner Creek Cafe RV Park with a lodge and bar.

50.5 Pullout on the left.

☆52.3 Bridge over the Dolores River and intersection with the West Dolores Road (7,640 feet) to the right. This magnificent, sun-dappled road leads 6.2 miles northwest to excellent camping at Marveeso Campground.

53.7 Large pullout near the sign "Leaving the San Juan National Forest." Things get hotter and less forested.

55.2 Fish hatchery.

58.3 Space to pull off the road. Access to a well-shaded spot on the river.

61.7 Large pullout on the left.

64.8 Dolores City Park, large but not really close to anything; no facilities or water.

★65.6 Flanders Park and City Center (6,980 feet) at the intersection with Fifth (Colorado Highway 145 here is Railroad Avenue), and the Dolores Visitors Information Center. The park is behind the library and is close to restaurants and a grocery store. You can even do some laundry in Dolores.

PASSES BY REGION

PASS	ELEVATION	DIFFICULTY
Northern Colorado		
Cameron	10,276 feet	East from Ted's Place 5, East from Tunnel 2, West 1
Rabbit Ears	9,426 feet	East 1, West 3
Trail Ridge Road High Point	12,183 feet	East 5, West 5
Willow Creek	9,620 feet	South 2, North 1
Gore	9,527 feet	East 2, West 2
Central Colorado		
Berthoud	11,315 feet	South 3, North 2
Squaw and Juniper	11,130 feet	East 4, West 1
Mount Evans	14,150 feet	North 5
Loveland	11,992 feet	East 1, West 3
Vail	10,600 feet	East 1, West 3
Kenosha and Red Hill	9,994 feet and 10,030 feet	East 3, West 1
Hoosier	11,541 feet	North 3, South 2
Fremont	11,318 feet	North 2, South 2
Tennessee	10,424 feet	North 3, South 1
Independence	12,095 feet	East 4, West 5
McClure	8,780 feet	North 2, South 1
Grand Mesa	10,840 feet	East 4, West 5

South-Central Colorado

Ute	9,165 feet	East 3, West 1
Wilkerson	9,507 feet	East 2, West 1
Trout Creek	9,487 feet	East 1, West 2
Cottonwood	12,126 feet	East 4
Poncha	9,019 feet	North 2, South 1
Monarch	11,312 feet	East 4, West 3
Hardscrabble	9,085 feet	East 3, West 1
North	10, 149 feet	East 3, West 2

Southern Colorado

Cucharas	9,941 feet	North 3, South 2
North La Veta	9,413 feet	East 2, West 2
Slumgullion and Spring Creek	11,530 feet and 10,901 feet	North 3, South 2
Wolf Creek	10,850 feet	North 3, South 5
La Manga and Cumbres	10,230 feet and 10,022 feet	North 3, South 3
Coal Bank and Molas	10,630 feet and 10,910 feet	South 5, North 2
Red Mountain	11,081 feet	South 2, North 5
Dallas Divide	8,970 feet	East 2, West 1
Lizard Head	10,250 feet	North 2, South 4

PASS-BAGGING LOG

DATE/PASS	NOTES
1.	
2.	
3.	
4.	
5.	
6.	
7.	
8.	

DATE/PASS	NOTES

9. _____

_____

10. _____

_____

11. _____

_____

12. _____

_____

13. _____

_____

14. _____

_____

15. _____

_____

16. _____

_____

17. _____

_____

DATE/PASS	NOTES

18. _____

_____

19. _____

_____

20. _____

_____

21. _____

_____

22. _____

_____

23. _____

_____

24. _____

_____

25. _____

_____

26. _____

_____

DATE/PASS	NOTES

27. _____

_____

28. _____

_____

29. _____

_____

30. _____

_____

31. _____

_____

32. _____

_____

33. _____

_____

34. _____

_____

35. _____

_____

DATE/PASS	NOTES

36. _____

_____

37. _____

_____

38. _____

_____

Index

About the Author

Photo by K. Stroffevkova.

An avid bicyclist, **KURT MAGSAMEN** began riding up and down the canyons southwest of Denver at age 16. A year later he completed his first 100-mile ride, and a few years after that he took off on a round-trip journey from Fort Collins to Yosemite Valley, on which he encountered quite a few passes. During the past 20 years, he has ridden over many more. He lives in Fort Collins, Colorado.

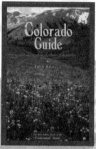